PRAISE FOR *LOVE REBELS*

"Getting involved in activism for the first time can feel intimidating; some veteran activists may seem unrelatable and even hostile to rookies. Kitty Stryker is the opposite of that—an activist with deep experience and a generous eagerness to welcome new folks to the good struggle. Now, with this book, everyone can feel like they have a wise older sibling guiding them on their radical journey. You will finish this book, as Stryker says, 'fertilized by curiosity and warmed by the light of compassion.'"
—Dr. Lisa Mueller, author of *The New Science of Social Change: A Modern Handbook for Activists*

"With the threat of Trumpian fascism mounting by the day, millions of people are looking for ways to become active and fight back. *Love Rebels* is the place to start. Its seamless blend of memoir, how-to, activist wisdom and poignant self-reflection provide an ideal blend for stimulating the kinds of difficult conversations necessary to construct durable communities of resistance to outlive MAGA."
—Mark Bray, author of *Antifa: The Anti-Fascist Handbook*

"Kitty Stryker has done it again. *Love Rebels* is a deeply personal, heartfelt chronicle of activism in our present age and an indispensable primer on getting involved on all levels: local, national and online. This inspiring, first-person account of grassroots organizing is desperately needed right now."
—Alex Winter, musician and actor, *Bill & Ted's Excellent Adventure*

"This book will teach you how to fight the good fight to the finish without destroying yourself in the process."
—Laurie Penny, journalist, political commentator and author of *Sexual Revolution: Modern Fascism and the Feminist Fightback*

"Artfully balancing personal anecdotes with incisive clarity and humor, Kitty Stryker is preparing a new generation of activists and organizers to take up the mantle and create our own ripples of change."
—Corrie Locke-Hardy, author of *The Revolution Will Be Well Fed : Recipes for Creating Community*

"*Love Rebels* offers practical advice for helping activists live and work productively alongside other humans, despite our flaws and peculiarities. It would be an important book at any time. But today, it's essential."
—Cathy Reisenwitz, Sex and the State

"Packed with practical guidance for those who are new to rebellion or nervous about direct action, as well as those of us who're exhausted from years of resistance. What makes this book extraordinary, though, is the loving generosity with which Kitty shares her own healing journey—an ongoing quest from burnout to boundaries and balance, with a healthy dose of accountability."
—Jenn Wilson, founder of the International Day of Consent

"*Love Rebels* offers a tender and insightful roadmap for all who are fighting to maintain their humanity while refusing to surrender their people and principles."
—Soraya Chemaly, author of *The Resilience Myth: New Thinking on Grit, Strength, and Growth after Trauma*

"*Love Rebels* does exactly what it says on the tin. It demystifies not just activism but accountability and how to handle it when you fall short of the mark."
—Riley Silverman, podcaster at *Good Chaotic* and head writer of *Troubled Waters*

LOVE REBELS

ALSO BY KITTY STRYKER

Ask Yourself: The Consent Culture Workbook

Say More: Consent Conversations for Teens

EDITED BY KITTY STRYKER

Ask: Building Consent Culture

KITTY STRYKER

LOVE REBELS

HOW I LEARNED TO BURN IT DOWN WITHOUT BURNING OUT

THORNAPPLE
PRESS

Love Rebels
How I Learned to Burn It Down Without Burning Out

Thornapple Press
300 – 722 Cormorant Street
Victoria, BC V8W 1P8 Canada
press@thornapplepress.ca

Our business offices are located on the traditional, ancestral and unceded territories of the lək̓ʷəŋən and W̱SÁNEĆ peoples. We return a percentage of company profits to the original stewards of this land through South Island Reciprocity Trust.

Thornapple Press is a brand of Talk Science to Me Communications Inc. Talk Science is a WBE Canada Certified Women Business Enterprise, a CGLCC Certified 2SLGBTQI+-owned business, and a Certified Living Wage Employer.

Cover illustration © 2025 by Jeffrey Werner
Cover and interior design by Jeffrey Werner
Substantive editing by Andrea Zanin
Copy-editing by Hazel Boydell
Proofreading by Alison Whyte
Index by Maria Hypponen

Library and Archives Canada Cataloging-In-Publication Data
Title: Love rebels : how I learned to burn it down without burning out / Kitty Stryker.
Names: Stryker, Kitty, 1984- author
Description: Includes bibliographical references and index.
Identifiers: Canadiana (print) 20250190710 | Canadiana (ebook) 20250191938 | ISBN 9781990869730 (softcover) | ISBN 9781990869747 (EPUB)
Subjects: LCSH: Activism. | LCSH: Activism—Psychological aspects. | LCSH: Interpersonal relations. | LCSH: Burn out (Psychology)— Prevention. | LCSH: Self-care, Health.
Classification: LCC HN18 .S79 2025 | DDC 303.48/4—dc23

10 9 8 7 6 5 4 3 2 1

Printed and bound in Canada by Friesens.

To you, and to us; to those who came before, and those who will come after. I love you.

The heart is a muscle the size of your fist.

Keep loving.

Keep fighting.

XXX

In the same way that your heart
feels and your mind thinks, you,
mortal beings, are the instrument
by which the universe cares.

If you choose to care, then
the universe cares.

If you don't, it doesn't.

—Brennan Lee Mulligan, *Dimension 20*

CONTENTS

FOREWORD

by carla joy bergman

Love Rebels is truly a remarkable book that I will return to often to help guide me through these accelerated and troubled times. My own book *Joyful Militancy: Building Thriving Resistance in Toxic Times* tackles some of the same themes in *Love Rebels*, but I did not anticipate how I would be challenged and humbled by this book. As I read, I found myself embracing some profound discomfort—I guess my growth edges were being poked at! By reading *Love Rebels*, I have gained knowledge and skills on how to move more ethically in my relationships and community, and for this alone I am grateful.

I knew it was solid from the start, when in the introduction Kitty writes, "It is useful to acknowledge that even people who talk, research and write about social justice or interpersonal relationships don't always have clear answers."

looks in mirror

Throughout the book there is a whisper that resonated through the pages (and maybe in part that came from our collective rebel ancestors): DON'T GIVE UP!

Before I began reading *Love Rebels,* I wrote in my notebook: *How can I write this at a time when I am rethinking everything I thought I believed in? In fact, I'm already burnt out!* The truth is, at this moment I am stuck in a cycle of despair and depression. Yet, when I opened the book, I immediately felt inspired and less alone. I was buoyed by Kitty's words: "Self-care is community care, and community care is self-care, like an ouroboros of mutual aid." We are entangled in beautifully complicated ways.

Kitty's vulnerability and openness to share her own story throughout *Love Rebels* makes for a brilliant book filled with concrete resources and strategies alongside personal memoir. She invites you into *her* world and offers her own stories of growth, mistakes and success. Alongside her personal stories are strategies and examples from other organizing movements, communities and people.

The book nudged me to notice that even amid my own burnout, I continue to show up for my friends and kin, and for strangers who call out for help across the rivers to the seas and onto the lands far from me—I hear the calls for solidarity, and I respond when and where I can. Is it because of *love* that I can still show up? I am not sure. I do know that even when despair has an enormous hold over me, I have always trusted that others will show up and do the work. Like Kitty, I have had a rebellious beating heart all my life, one that yearns to get together with my friends and compose better worlds together, to trust each other, to find pockets of joy, and to love.

Yet, trusting and loving and feeling trusted and loved under capitalism is bloody hard! Capitalism stokes competition and individualism, and transactional ways of relating are smuggled into our communities and friendships, causing all of us harm. It takes a fierce resolve and commitment to be otherwise, but it is the foundational work. Capitalist and colonial ways of relating make us feel hollow and never enough; they can be incredibly violent and tear our communities apart.

Kitty not only shows an alternative way through these harmful ideologies and structures; she also gives us concrete steps on how to nurture a mutuality of love in all our relationships, including and especially with ourselves. She does this by sharing her own moments of burnout and feelings of lack alongside examples of how she humbly found her way through those times. She points to how even when collective struggles and interpersonal conflicts flash up, there are ways to get through them, especially when we arm ourselves with good faith in others. The stories and examples in this book encourage a profound trust in Kitty as a guide—because she does not shy away from sharing that she too is flawed and can make mistakes.

Love Rebels is welcoming, friendly, funny and fierce. Throughout the book, Kitty invites us to take what we need and leave the rest behind, because love and rebellion are both incredibly personal and intrinsically interwoven with the needs of community. We are given ways to ask ourselves questions and to dig further into our own knowings. Kitty moves towards trouble with grace and embraces the messiness inherent in all relationships. She is committed to finding ways together to work it out—which includes sometimes severing ties.

I am writing this foreword at a time when fascism is undeniably surging globally, amid ongoing genocides and with continual wars popping off. But there are the activists and everyday people who are on the brink of a massive uprising that will stretch across the world. In the US, despite their differences, people are taking to the streets with a fierce resolve to stop Immigration and Customs Enforcement (ICE) from kidnapping their children and community members. These are not only activists in the traditional sense, but regular folks who are coming out in large numbers, putting their bodies in the line of fire. If these brave acts of solidarity aren't love and rebellion, I don't know what is!

There is no question to anyone who is paying attention that we are in apocalyptic times. We don't know what the future holds, so we need more guides, ideas and examples of ways to get through. Sharing our stories, like Kitty has done in *Love Rebels,* helps us come together, not only to fight against the horrors, but to carve out ways to also fight *for what* and *whom we love!* There are many front lines, and some are subtle and under the radar. People are doing work that we will never know about but that will be profoundly felt by many one day. I try to hold on gently to the notion that nothing is permanent, including fascism. As love rebels, we have the fortitude and the passion to do this together! But we need each other so we can find new landscapes in the rubble.

No matter where you are on the path towards collective freedom, there's something for you in this book. We all have growth edges to contend with, and we are all still learning. *Love Rebels* is a powerful invitation to find our way amid struggle and activism without doing more harm to ourselves or each other—to embrace our imperfections and mistakes with responsibility and good faith. Let's continue to love and care for ourselves and for others, to rest when we need to and to not forget to have fun doing it!

You are not alone. You are loved. And as Kitty says, "There are plenty of things to do, and they'll still be there tomorrow."

carla joy bergman

On the lands of the Lekwungen-speaking peoples of the Songhees Nation and Xʷsepsəm Nation, and w̱SÁNEĆ peoples. Victoria, Canada, June 2025

ACKNOWLEDGMENTS

I wouldn't be able to focus so much of my time on writing about social justice, compassionate activism, healthy accountability and more if it wasn't for the amazing support system I have around me.

Thank you to my dad, Justin, and my mum, Amanda, for raising me to care fiercely about the world and empowering me to be the change I want to see in the world.

Thank you to AV and Avens, for being my best friends, the (Biblical) angel and (silver-tongued) devil on my shoulders, gently nudging me into being my absolute best while also loving my trash panda self.

Thank you to my friends Miriam, Colin, Kiera and Cheapendale's Ranch for listening to me gnash my teeth as I chewed over the content of this book.

Thank you to my publisher, Thornapple Press, for constantly believing in my passion and letting me write what needs to come out. Thank you also to Andrea Zanin and Hazel Boydell for giving me the time and the structure to make this the best possible thing it could be.

Thank you to my Patreon patrons, who fund me year-round so I can focus on my writing instead of panicking about rent.

Thank you to my mentee for opening my mind to a world I had little knowledge of and for teaching me to be patient and kind instead of quick to dismiss and judge.

Thank you to so many activists who have helped shape my understanding of community activism in its many forms: Wagatwe Wanjuki, Elle Armageddon, Carol Queen, Trần Xuân Thu, Kim Kelly, Patrick Califia, Julia Serano, Shane Burley, Mya Byrne, Chuck Tingle, Talia Lavin, Beau of the Fifth Column, Shane Lukas, Brennan Lee Mulligan, Rebecca Solnit and so many more—I could fill up a book with names. And thank you to Dalia Sapon-Shevin for the woodcut she created for the 1999 WTO protests, which inspired the words in the second half of my dedication as well as so much other art.

And of course, thank you to my cats and the crows, who made sure I maintained a schedule and fed myself—*after* I fed them.

INTRODUCTION

I was born to be an activist.

As a toddler, I went to NOW rallies and Take Back the Night with my parents, wearing a pin that said, "I'm a mini feminist." It wasn't long before I added environmentalism to my ever-increasing list of causes. I wrote a strongly worded letter to Bill Clinton when I was around ten, explaining that the ozone layer was a serious issue and we needed to get on top of it quickly. I remember the day I got a letter back, and how thrilled I was—until I opened the envelope to find a form letter signed in printer ink and an oversized trading card with Clinton's face on it. I realized that writing to the president was like shouting into an abyss, and I burned that shit.

That was the day I lost faith in bipartisan politics and became an anarchist. Instead of looking to elected officials to get things done, I threw myself into direct action. I stopped expecting other people to do what was needed and empowered myself to do that work instead. I cleaned up trash in my neighborhood with the Recycling Committee. I started my school's Gay Straight Alliance. I marched—alone—with a sign demanding LGBTQ+ rights in a parade celebrating the town I lived in (to be fair, that was in part because I didn't realize that when the town said pride parade, they meant civic pride, not gay pride). If I saw injustice, I felt that it was on me to fix it.

I was not always compassionate about my activism, mind. Sometimes I was a little too quick to snipe at "the enemy." My grandma told me about how, when I was a child, I was protecting a local Planned Parenthood clinic from anti-abortion activists. Apparently, I saw another kid about my age with a sign that said, "by chance not by choice." I marched right up to him and said innocently, "Oh, you weren't a choice? I was a choice." And I just walked away, unaware that I was presumably leaving that poor kid with something to process in therapy years later. It was not the approach I would take today!

I don't remember these early incidents that well, but I do remember sobbing my eyes out throughout my childhood and teenager years because the world already seemed like a dark and hopeless place. There were so many fronts to fight in, and as my world expanded, so did the causes I cared about. This continues to be true even as I enter my 40s. I discover new horrors every day and resolve to be in solidarity with those fighting them.

GROWING AS AN ACTIVIST

My childhood fervor continued as I became an adult. I entered sex work in my early 20s, and very quickly became involved with the Sex Workers Outreach Project, arguing for decriminalization as a safer option for many sex workers and protesting PayPal for shutting down sex worker accounts. Doing sex work rights activism inspired me to explore issues with the economy in more depth, and that research is part of what inspired me to train as a medic during Occupy Wall Street. As I read and educated myself, the destructive interactions between class, race and capitalism were fresh fuel. It no longer felt like enough to write essays, to organize, to protest. I wanted to help those who were putting their bodies on the line for what they believed in.

When I started working as a medic, I learned basic first aid and how to recognize dehydration, which was incredibly useful at protests. I began carrying supplies in my purse because I never knew when it might come in handy to have sterile gauze, antibiotic ointment and duct tape. Turns out, it was incredibly useful most of the time! I became that "mom friend" who could be counted on to have supplies, from ibuprofen for headaches to naloxone for opioid overdoses. Treating a burn or a knee scrape became second nature.

As I grew more skilled, I would get asked for help with situations that weren't quite bad enough for urgent care, but that needed some kind of care. Many of the people seeking me out didn't have health insurance and, without my help, might have injured themselves further. I was always quick to remind people that I was not a doctor, but for many, the choice was between my medic training and nothing at all. I learned crisis and de-escalation skills, and helped people in crisis seek appropriate and accessible mental health care as best I could. I helped friends who were terrified of state facilities get through withdrawal, and if it got beyond my skill set, I stayed with them at the hospital as an advocate and company. I became a bit of a first aid nerd, and even an amateur herbalist.

It was Gamergate that changed my attitude towards activism from a proud civic duty to a grim determination. As many non-men online have experienced, the internet can be an incredibly hostile place, from online bullying to rape and death threats. This is even more true if you deign to write about traditionally "nerdy" things like *Star Wars,* Dungeons and Dragons and video games. Gamergate was a loosely organized, right-wing leaning, misogynist hate campaign that started in earnest in 2014. An angry man wrote a blog post in which he accused his ex-partner, video game developer Zoë Quinn, of getting a favorable review thanks to Zoë's sexual relationship with the reviewer. That blog post was shared to the cesspool online forum 4Chan as proof of corruption in the video game industry, and #Gamergate became a hashtag for white men to complain about the "wokeness" that had invaded their consoles. Gamergaters were notorious for harassing women and nonbinary people in games in the name of "ethics in game journalism." Many of the names that rose to prominence in the chaos—Milo Yiannopoulos, for example, who became Gamergate's figurehead—soon found themselves with new fans and opportunities amongst the developing "alt-right."

When Gamergate began, I was dating a trans woman who was part of a community that developed indie games, but I didn't make them myself. I didn't even play video games. Even so, I got caught up in the fury of 4Channers, who doxxed me (releasing what they considered to be my legal name, home address, phone number, even my parents' address) on KiwiFarms (another online forum, specifically created to share the personal information of targets for the purposes of harassment) for daring to date an indie video game developer. Even worse, in their eyes, was that she was a trans woman. It was scary. For the first time, I considered whether to get a gun license, though I chose not to. Activism no longer felt like a choice, but a necessity.

While I had learned a little bit about street medic work while occasionally showing up at protests or at Occupy encampments, Gamergate made me feel a lot more determined to speak up and provide material support. When my home address was released online and strangers gloated about their plans to attack me, it only made me feel grimly resolute in my activism. Many of the up-and-coming white supremacist, chauvinist and Christian nationalist figureheads who were grouped together as the "alt-right" teethed in online forums dedicated to Gamergate. People like Milo Yiannopoulos, Adam Baldwin and Mike Cernovich rose to prominence by attacking marginalized people in the name of "ethics in game journalism," and were elevated into positions of influence by right-wing figures such as Steve Bannon, a founder of Breitbart News. Soon, aspiring troll-in-chief Donald Trump took notice and reached a welcoming hand out to the people and tactics of the alt-right. From there, he bullied his way into the presidency.

Aware of the damage the alt-right was capable of, I knew I had to push back. What started as a casual interest in protest medicine became a large part of my activism. I began going out to protests, from anti-Trump demonstrations to Black Lives Matter marches, as a street medic. While I was initially going out with a focus on hydration and treating sprains, I quickly realized in the run-up to Trump's first presidency that I had to learn an array of new, terrifying skills: how to treat the effects of tear gas, how to handle someone's bleeding head while ducking for cover, how to persuade a crowd of scared people to walk instead of run when the cops were shooting "less lethals" at them (running often leads to chaos, with people tripping and hurting themselves—you want folks to walk for wider safety). I became horrifyingly aware that I might find myself in a situation where I had to help stabilize someone while waiting for the EMTs. I had always known the cops weren't my friends, particularly as a sex worker, and I wasn't surprised to learn how often the alt-right and the police were the same people. Now I had to worry about the police shooting at me for being an identifiable medic or harassing me at home if neo-Nazis doxxed me, trying to pump me for information on other protesters.

The night that Trump was elected in 2016, my partners and I left an election night gathering to march in the streets. We didn't know we would be out there for hours every day for days on end. We choked on tear gas and pepper spray, nursed our bruises and sore muscles, and re-upped medical supplies to be available to go out at any time. There wasn't a break from activism, only time in the streets protesting, and time at home strategizing. 4Chan quickly became an online recruitment funnel into violent alt-right street militias like the Proud Boys and 3 Percenters, and white nationalist groups like Identity Evropa and the Ku Klux Klan. Even when we weren't out in the streets, my fellow activists and I had to be alert at all times, not only for our own safety but the safety of our friends and families.

Meanwhile, mainstream media dismissed what left-leaning activists were experiencing—as they often did with marginalized people—painting us as just as bad as the people we were fighting against. My partners and I were increasingly aware that we not only had to trust each other as lovers, but as comrades in a culture war. It was incredibly stressful and there was no real escape or time out. I began smoking and drinking in earnest because I had to snatch what pleasure I could from out of the gaping maw of The Work, while my partners found their own escape mechanisms. Disagreements about tactics were not intellectual exercises. Instead, they were really about how much we could trust each other with our physical safety or even things like our legal names. It was a type of hell that destroyed our ability to relate kindly to each other and eventually isolated us. I'm pretty sure that was the point of all the chaos the alt-right was bringing all along.

RETHINKING WHAT PROTEST IS

To the horror of many in my community, and most people around the world, Trump was re-elected for a second term. He had said more than once that if he were elected, he would do everything he could to send us into an authoritarian theocracy and I believe him, if the January 6, 2021, attack on the Capitol by Trump's followers is anything to go by. After almost fifty years of work by the religious right, Roe vs. Wade, a 1973 case that legalized abortion in the US, was overturned in June 2022. The strides we've made for LGBTQ+ rights are being undone all across the country, to the point that people are trying to figure out their escape strategies from the United States if they have the financial privilege to do so. Project 2025, a blatant strategy for turning the United States into a Christofascist country, is being enacted on multiple fronts while Democratic leadership calls, bewilderingly, for civility in the face of hostility. Civil service workers are being replaced by people loyal to Trump. Under the guide of "efficiency," Elon Musk is being given full reign over federal agencies he doesn't understand the intricacies of, like the Center for Disease Control or the Federal Aviation Administration. Immigration and Customs Enforcement and the Department of Homeland Security are deporting legal residents and leaving thousands of others in detention without due process. It's overwhelming and scary. Not a day goes by without a friend messaging me to ask, "Is this the collapse of the US?"

While I live in the United States and my own concerns tend to start at home, authoritarianism is on the rise everywhere. The International Institute for Democracy and Electoral Assistance said in 2022 that "the number of countries moving towards authoritarianism is more than double those moving towards democracy and that authoritarian regimes worldwide have deepened their repression, with 2021 being the worst year on record."[1] At the time of writing, Russia is still attacking Ukraine while Trump humiliates President Zelenskyy during diplomatic discussions. Iran is using the death penalty and public floggings to quash dissent. There are mass killings in Congo. Israel is bombing Gaza into dust, with American politicians on both sides of the aisle funding the destruction and much of the international community looking on impassively. Things are dire, and fascism is on the rise.

It's been over five years since I last went out into the streets to serve as a medic. This is in part because of a physical disability that was aggravated when I pushed myself too hard, and in part because of trauma. I injured myself in 2019 and needed to take a break from working as a street medic on call, and then the COVID-19 pandemic kept me away. Instead, I found ways to support the front lines from home. Even so, it took me until 2023 to be able to sleep soundly at night without waking up in a sweat, panicking about Proud Boys trying to beat me down or gasping for breath, thinking I was choking on tear gas. I now have a carbon fiber walking stick next to my door because it makes me feel safer—it's nearly indestructible and a useful tool if I need to defend myself. I no longer keep a full medic bag in my trunk, but I do have some assorted first aid supplies with me at all times. If this is how I feel as a white, cis activist, I can't imagine the constant anxiety humming in the guts of my friends who are Black and brown, trans and nonbinary. It is for them I would take up my medic bag again,

---

1   The Global State of Democracy 2022, International Institute for Democracy and Electoral Assistance, https://www.idea.int/democracytracker/sites/default/files/2022-11/the-global-state-of-democracy-2022.pdf

but quite honestly, I dread it. I have seen people stabbed at a rally, watched video of people shot for protesting and read about people mowed down in cars when marching. I don't feel proud of my willingness to keep fighting back against violent white supremacy as much as I feel exhausted by the necessity.

And yet, I haven't been inactive in those five years away from the streets. I have found many ways to contribute: offering jail support and raising bail money for other protestors, writing articles that increase awareness about consent and teaching others how to stay level-headed in a crisis. I have learned how to listen when called out on my bullshit and how to access fierce compassion when I am the one calling someone on theirs. I have reminded people that movements need all kinds of people with all sorts of skills, from direct action to lobbying to fundraising to childcare. Most importantly, I think, I have held space for vulnerability, for people who are doing this incredibly difficult and unending anti-oppression work to have a moment to say, "This sucks, actually." In these five years, I have been volunteering at an animal shelter while advocating for unhoused people and their pets. I have been mentoring an evangelical teen while he goes through a crisis of faith and learns how to think critically. I've organized my neighbors to be collectively prepared for natural disasters.

I believe strongly that activism comes in many forms. While protesting in the streets or engaging in big direct actions is one type of activism (and usually what the media focuses on when they talk about "activism"), it's almost always just one piece of a much bigger pie. I've seen angry debates on tactics between people who have very different ideas on what activism "should" be. More often than not, the answer is that we need more of all of it, in every form! Every movement I can think of has involved a diverse cross-section of people and skills. Therefore, I think it can undermine the building of strong coalitions to put just one kind of activism on a pedestal. This is part of why I am trying, in my mind and in my writing, to widen the idea of protest and direct action to not only mean marching in the streets or blocking access to a bridge (though those things are part of it). These terms, in my mind, also apply to more subtle forms of protest, such as making LGBTQ+ books accessible to youth through free libraries or feeding unhoused people. Both of these actions may be illegal, depending on where you live, but are less visibly disruptive to the status quo than more commonly agreed forms of protest or direct action.

Sweeping social change has always taken the whole village. We need people on the front lines, sure, but we also need people to write letters to their local representatives, people to provide bail support, folks to offer childcare so parents can protest, others to offer legal support and host fundraisers and more experienced activists to train others on de-escalation, self-defense and street medic skills. We need non-violent demonstrations, and we need community defense leagues. We need people who focus on voting rights and access, and people who offer survival-related mutual aid. We need soup kitchens and free boxes. We need dog runs for homeless shelters. We need people with progressive ideas to run for local government. We need out gay politicians like Harvey Milk and we need disruptive actions that draw attention to causes like ACT-UP did for AIDS. We need inspiring speakers like Angela Davis, and we need community-minded revolutionaries like Huey Newton.

Activism in any form is not always comfortable or fun, and it does come at a risk. I think we are long past the point where it's reasonable to simply hope "this too shall pass." I wrote this book in the hope of strengthening people who were faltering with their gas tank on empty, to let them know they aren't alone. I also wrote it to inspire people who are nervous about offline activism—I hope they will be able to gain some useful tools and resources that empower them to take that next step away from the keyboard. From teens to elders, we need *everyone* to show up, in person, in their communities! That unity is powerful stuff.

CREATING COALITION

I've been an educator specifically around concepts of consent—what it means, how to do it, and what gets in the way—for most of my adult life. I was raised to be very confident in my bodily autonomy thanks to my parents, who taught me about feminism and reproductive rights. Consent is certainly another layer to that. But as I grew older and learned about the ways LGBTQ+ people have been policed around how they can dress in public or what they're allowed to talk about at work or in school, I realized that consent isn't just about sex and reproduction. And as I learned about the ways that Black folks have had their consent violated in the name of medicine, I realized it wasn't just about romantic relationships, either. In fact, the more I learned about oppression and injustice, the more I saw the tendrils of consent violations everywhere—in residential schools that forcibly separated Indigenous children from their families, in dangerous workplaces that flout safety laws, in the prison system's treatment of incarcerated people. So many causes and struggles are connected by the root network of consent.

When my book *Ask: Building Consent Culture* was released, one of the reviews said I patted myself on the back for making a point of ensuring that the anthology prioritized the voices of marginalized people. That review hurt my feelings and made me at war within myself. A guilty, "They're right, I shouldn't even be saying anything about my process, who do I think I am?" clashed into a defensive, "All I was trying to do was offer a blueprint for others to do the same thing, isn't that good?" It took a while for me to realize that both reactions ultimately centered on me and whether I was recognized for the work I was doing. The truth, as it often is, is probably in the middle—I likely could have framed my intention better and less smugly, and also my intention was a genuine and heartfelt one.

Someone may look at this intro and scoff that my decision to tell the story of my own journey into activism is tooting my own horn. But I've learned that that's OK. There is no one right way that will speak to absolutely everyone, and my approach isn't inherently wrong. It's worthwhile to humbly listen to criticism and take it in good faith. I can lose so much time and energy trying to persuade someone who just doesn't like me that I am likable and A Good Person, but that's energy I'd rather spend volunteering on projects that better my community. I can choose to learn from criticism, even when it's meant to be hurtful, and *I can keep doing the work*. Perfect is the enemy of done, and I won't let the fear of getting it wrong stop me from trying to leave the world a bit better than I found it.

When I initially started thinking about this book and about what I wanted to say as I stared down the barrel of an election year that seemed doomed in a thousand different ways, I disassociated.[2] I became avoidant. I suddenly became very interested in remodeling my garden, volunteering with a three-legged dog picnic and making a faux guillotine out of

---

2   In this book, I use the American Psychiatric Association definition of dissociation as a "disconnection between a person's thoughts, memories, feelings, actions or sense of who they are" and disassociation as separating and disconnecting from certain elements of an experience. The first is a trauma response and the second a coping mechanism, especially when someone is feeling overwhelmed.

cardboard scraps for my cat's birthday, which is also Bastille Day. I second-guessed myself—after all, who am I to write a book about activist burnout? I'm not an academic. I'm not a therapist. I'm just a person who probably needs this book as much as the person reading it.

However, I came to the conclusion that many things aren't done by the person who is ideal for the job. They're done by imperfect people who are struggling to figure out a way forward. They're done by people who stumble and get it wrong sometimes. It would be great if we could delegate every task to the perfect person, but what we have is simply ourselves, trying to figure it out as best we can.

This book is about recognizing that the people around you are, for the most part, probably acting in good faith and are doing what they think is the right thing to do. That's a difficult thing to swallow when we disagree on what is ethical. But for the health of my heart (in both a spiritual and literal sense), in the last couple of years I have found myself stopping before I wade into yet another online argument and instead asking myself, "To what end?" What is my goal, and is this the most effective way to achieve it? More often than not, I have realized that the answer is no—I don't need to weigh in. Instead, I take a deep breath and delete my rant. I realized at some point that I needed to find a better way to fight my battles, to find some commonality, to humanize others and, in turn, get them to humanize me.

There is a tension, of course. I do believe in the tolerance paradox: that tolerating intolerance leads to more intolerance. You can't tolerate Nazis—they will only multiply. But so many groups of people aren't Nazis, they are people that I can ride to the next bus stop with. Sure, I am probably going to disagree with what the federal government should look like when discussing it with a friend who is a Democratic Socialist and a friend who is a libertarian. But we can work together on other things, like finding ways to help unhoused people and ending qualified immunity for police officers.

I think there are ways for people with different political viewpoints to work together, and that it requires a willingness to embrace nuance. It sometimes requires biting your tongue and sometimes requires standing up for what you believe in. It often requires recognizing that perfect is the enemy of done, and that "done" can be a matter of life and death for many. Coalition building and cooperation often mean we have to stand on the tightrope woven from a bunch of different warring ideals and find our balance while we settle the anxieties that bubble up. It's scary, but it's also a skillset, and you can learn the flexibility that makes it easier.

It is useful to acknowledge that even people who talk, research and write about social justice or interpersonal relationships don't always have clear answers. We're all wounded animals stumbling through the brush, trying to have a healthy balance between our beliefs, our work and those we care about. You are a wounded animal, and so are they. So are we all.

I was so nervous sitting down to write this book. I would laugh to my friends, "I'm writing a book about how to have radical relationships while doing radical activism and not losing your mind. When I figure out how to do it, I'll let you know!" But when I finally stopped avoiding it, I found the words came easily. I'm never going to say that I have The Answer. But I can say I've had a lot of the same questions that you may have, and this book details the tools I used to come to a place of equilibrium.

I was inspired to write this book after many years of reflection on the difficulties of being an activist in relationships with others—family, friends, comrades, coworkers. As a part of that, I've been reading a lot about how people get wrapped up in things like the right-wing, anti-Semitic conspiracy of QAnon, a religious cult like Jonestown, the science denialism of anti-vaccination or the transphobia of "gender-critical feminism." For many years, I didn't spend a lot of time wondering why people were attracted to ideologies that encourage a lack of critical thinking to create a stark "you're either with us or against us." I just shut people out of my life if they were invested in those ideologies—a valid response, for sure. Over the last five years, however, I have explored the many ways that fear of what isn't understood, a need to be right and a desire to not be alone cause people to flock to belief systems with simple, black-and-white answers. I've learned a lot about how these groups weaponize curiosity and doubt and threaten isolation for those who question those simplistic answers.

While I'm still horrified at the things done in the name of these ideologies, I understand them a little better. More importantly, I've stopped thinking of myself as above the people who hurt others in the name of their beliefs. I can see the ways that the us vs. them tendency happens in the groups I identify with. Anarchists vs. communists vs. libertarians, for example. In these interactions, the people waging battles often speak more than they listen. We also have a desire for cleanly defined victims and perpetrators, and that is another way we do harm. I see it in how people use social justice language as a cudgel to prevent discussion, whether they do so in good faith or not. I'm still trying to unpack the ways in which I, too, fall into these oversimplified dichotomies without noticing.

THE SCOPE OF THIS BOOK

Love Rebels went through a few different phases before coming into being as what you hold in your hands. I knew that trying to write a simple "how to" guide was not only too expansive—there are as many ways to be an activist as there are people in the world—but also, in a world increasingly given over to fascism, it could be seen as some kind of dangerous manifesto and be used as an excuse to further harass me and my loved ones. I also didn't want to write something that was pure memoir, because I think I have some lessons to impart from what I've picked up over the years. I realized that what I do best is illustrate the tensions that may occur when activism is near and dear to our hearts and provide tools to help ease those tensions. I never want to suggest my experience is the only real experience, or that my advice is the be-all, end-all. Rather, this book is packed full of musings, lessons and tricks I've learned in a lifetime of radical activism. I talk about both successes and mistakes. It is not intended to be a foolproof guidebook that will help you have perfect outcomes in every activist coalition and personal relationship. Rather, my hope is that *Love Rebels* will serve as a comfort and a friend when you feel stressed and confused. This is like me listening to you over the phone when you feel like you're about to burn out. I want this to feel like a friend who has been through it too, giving your shoulder a squeeze and saying, "Hey, it's OK, you're not alone."

I've arranged these chapters from the personal to the organizational, but keep in mind that all of these things are linked so you may find advice in the more individually focused chapters that helps you with an organizational issue or vice versa.

The early chapters define terms, wrestle with the power disparities that influence how we relate to each other and talk about how to take care of ourselves while caring for others. Then, I talk about how to embrace accountability and how to find equilibrium with our families (whether we do activism with them or not) and give a brief overview of the different types of activism. Finally, I dig into figuring out and discussing risk assessment with loved ones and what healthy leadership can look like (both as a community member and as a leader). I ask questions at the end of each chapter to encourage you to figure out what you personally care about and want to manifest in the world. I want to promote self-reflection, to gently and firmly ask you to consider, "What am I afraid of? How can I acknowledge that fear? How can I find ways to show up bravely without destroying myself in the process?"

This book is a love letter to my fellow bleeding-heart humans who want to give everything they can to their causes but who are also losing themselves in the process. I want to offer a hand and say, "I see you drowning, and I think there might be a better way." Being a love rebel is about loving fiercely, but also loving sustainably. Understanding and loving ourselves is the core of our strength.

Take what serves you and leave the rest—this is meant to stimulate your mind and make you think about your own experience in new ways, rather than tell you what to do or how to feel! Thank you for being a love rebel with me.

PART ONE:
GET GROUNDED

CHAPTER 1:
WHAT IS A LOVE REBEL, ANYWAY?

The best place to start any conversation, in my experience, is to define terms and frameworks so we're all on the same page. Once we establish the container in which we're working, we can more easily understand how to have a productive discussion.

WHAT IS RADICAL ACTIVISM?

I often see people online treating activism as if there are only two approaches: direct action against the establishment through protests and occupation or working alongside the establishment by voting or writing letters. Especially in the United States, these strategies are pitted against each other, with those working with the system telling proponents of direct action that they're too hostile, and those working against the system telling letter writers that they're too complacent. One certainly comes off as more "radical" than the other if we define radical as meaning "working to bring change through high-risk activities." Certainly, that's how the media chooses to frame direct action—as "violent" and "disruptive."

But I wonder if we could expand the idea of a radical framework to embrace more. I wonder if this divide between activism that is deemed "respectable" and that considered "radical" is promoted by politicians to create an intentional rift between two strategies that, when combined, have been responsible for most of the drastic social changes we've seen.

Black anti-racist activist and prison abolitionist Angela Davis said in her book *Women, Culture, and Politics*:

> If we are not afraid to adopt a revolutionary stance—if, indeed, we wish to be radical in our quest for change—then we must get to the root of our oppression. After all, radical simply means "grasping things at the root."

In defining radicalism this way, we can begin to see the importance of speaking out against injustice in the streets, at a ballot box and everywhere in between.

When I talk to people about activism and ask them if they're an activist, some people hem and haw about whether or not what they do "counts." I'll admit, it's something I still grapple with, as I believe strongly that people should show up in the ways that are sustainable for them, and yet I also carry some judgment if I feel that people aren't showing up *enough* (and I judge myself for this too). I suspect social media has had a role to play here, where the loudest actions often get the most attention. I also think that the media has fixated on radical activists being scary, chaotic and violent, to such an extent that it spreads conspiracies about philanthropic people like George Soros funding black-clad anarchists. This focus not only makes quieter types of activism invisible, but it also ignores that many people are unable to do high-risk actions. But quieter activists and their contributions are no less vital, even if they may hesitate to label it as activism themselves.

This struggle is a deeply personal one for me. I remember during one period of social unrest where I felt guilty for not going out in the streets as a medic. I was having increased physical pain, I didn't have anyone to be my protest buddy, which made me feel uncomfortable, and there was a pandemic sweeping across the world. But I still felt like I should be pushing myself to be out there, because the issue was one that deeply mattered to me. If I cared, shouldn't I be doing more?

After some reflection, though, I realized that not only was I physically unable to be out there for the time it could take, but I was still dealing with trauma from the last time I had worked as a street medic for weeks on end. I was not in a stable enough physical or emotional state to be on the streets, and being out there could be not only a risk for me but a liability for others. In-person activism is part of my lifeblood, so not feeling capable of marching in the streets felt disappointing, even as I knew that it was the right long-term decision. I also realized that there were many other ways I could contribute from home, so I did that instead. I monitored police scanners during protests and communicated to people on the ground what the police were planning as best I could, so protesters could maneuver more effectively. I offered safe rides to people who were ready to leave protests. I signal-boosted bail funds and contributed to fundraisers. I cooked meals for tired protesters so they could rest and recover. All of those things were as important as being on the front line because they created sustainable resilience and community care. Those things are also activism, even if it took me a while to understand them as such.

Let's consider another example. I think that empowering disenfranchised voters is a radical act. Fighting arbitrary restrictions on absentee ballots, redistricting, gerrymandering and photo ID laws are vital. When Black and brown folks are convicted of felonies at much higher rates and thus robbed of their votes in some states, voting itself becomes direct action.

Similarly, writing strongly worded letters may feel like a fool's errand, but the anti-abortion lobby uses this technique to effectively intimidate politicians into supporting their agenda all the time. Many legislators recognize that people who feel strongly enough to write a letter are also people who feel engaged enough to vote. Can a good letter change a politician's mind all by itself? It's unlikely, but that letter can be an indication of which way the wind is blowing, and what it symbolizes can be influential.

I see plenty of news articles decrying occupations as more nuisance than political statement or hinting that activists who blockade a road shouldn't be surprised if they get run over, as that blockade is inherently aggressive. Yet physical protests have been effective at creating lasting change when voting and letters have not. One such case was in April 1977, when disability activists staged a month-long sit-in at multiple Health, Education, and Welfare (HEW) offices to push for the signing and enforcement of Section 504 of the Rehabilitation Act of 1973 (which recognized disability as a civil rights category). Section 504 offered access to education and employment for people with disabilities, but it had been a law for four years without any enforcement. The sit-ins ensured that the activists could not be ignored any longer, while also creating bonds between different groups in the fight for disability access: the Black Panthers and their fight for Black civil rights, Glide Memorial Church and their fight for gay rights, and the International Association of Machinists with their fight for union rights. Twenty-six days later, the increase in pressure from the media due to coverage of the sit-ins pushed Secretary Joseph A Califano, Jr. to finally sign the regulations for Section 504 of the 1973 Rehabilitation Act.

My point here is that both "quiet" and more attention-grabbing types of political engagement have been useful throughout the years to create change, and they often bounce off each other to keep up momentum. Yet, they are often pitted against each other, encouraged to decry one or the other as less effective or even useless. And, in that bitter argument, we forget the multitude of strategies that exist between the two: mutual aid networks, providing free childcare to protesters, raising money for bail bonds, etc. A holistic approach that tackles the root cause of injustice while also relieving the symptoms is needed to make activism both radical and sustainable.

It's also important to consider that there are many reasons why people may feel unwilling to attend a protest. Being immunosuppressed means risking physical repercussions, and many neurodivergent people may find large crowds too overwhelming. An immigrant or undocumented person may feel that the risk of an arrest and subsequent legal consequences outweighs their desire to attend. Trans and nonbinary people have a much harder time when arrested and are at increased risk for violence from police. The same is overwhelmingly true for Black and brown people. People with mobility concerns may feel afraid of being left behind or being targeted by police violence (a not unreasonable fear). A person with dependents may not be able to risk the financial hit of missing shifts or losing their job as a result of attending a protest. A person also might just not want to take part in a protest, despite feeling strongly about the cause. Any of these reasons are good enough, and not being on the front lines doesn't mean you aren't a true activist, or that you don't care enough.

So, what is radical activism? I like the definition of radical as seeking to transform society through social change, structural change, revolution and reform. I think it's different from extremism because radicalism is idealistic at the core—it seeks to hear more people and liberate all, rather than creating freedom for a selected group. In my definition of radical activism, violence is sometimes unavoidable but is not sought out, while extremism tends to thrive on the fear violence creates. I say all this with a wry smile, because I know that everyone thinks their values are radical and not extremist, so who can really define it without bias?

I'm an anarchosyndicalist. In a very quick and dirty summary that means that I believe in the freedom of anarchy with the structure of unions and cooperative business models instead of government oversight. I particularly care about mutual aid, which is when people take care of each other on a community basis, sharing resources and services voluntarily and with core values of solidarity and reciprocity. I have generally veered towards that approach as an initial framework to address many of the social problems I see. Feeding my unhoused neighbors is a form of radical activism, and I see being a sobriety buddy for people in my community as a form of radical activism too. Mentoring a gay evangelical teen is just as much radical activism as being a street medic and volunteering at an animal shelter. I could do all of these mutual aid activities from a variety of political positions, and so, I wouldn't define radical activism as affiliated with any political viewpoint. Many of the stories in here are from my leftist point of view, but I recognize that my version of radical is not the only one.

In understanding my framework for this book, it is important to recognize that I see radicalism as more than just a label or a brand. It is a way of seeing the world and informing our actions within it. It's about being in solidarity with marginalized people, not a one-time gesture. It is a constant state of learning and growing and changing. Everything I believe today comes from layers of feminism and Black liberation and gay rights and environmental battles and accessibility activism and Marx and Foucault and even Sir Terry Pratchett. Perhaps that's part of what makes radicalism so beautiful to me—how optimistic and amorphous it can be. It's like the "yes, and?" of activism.[3]

WHAT MAKES A RELATIONSHIP RADICAL?

When I was a teenager, I defined a radical relationship as a romantic one in which the dynamic was somehow radical in the eyes of the mainstream, a challenge to the status quo. Maybe that was a declared power dynamic like Dominance/submission, or perhaps it was a nonmonogamous relationship. This framework led me to ask some questions: Is a queer relationship radical in its very nature? What about a relationship between people who share a political ideology? Could one person bring a radical approach into a relationship regardless of the other person?

Yeah, I'm an overthinker.

Then, I started to unpack why the label of "radical" felt meaningful to me. One way I interrogated that impulse was

---

3   "Yes, and?" is a concept taken from improvisational comedy that suggests that an improviser should accept what another has said and then expand on it. The principle has been adopted in other circles as a way of fostering effective communication and improving idea sharing.

to think about my relationship to the word "queer." I identify as queer in part because it works as shorthand for "not heterosexual," but also because there is an unspoken awareness that the word has been used as a slur, and by choosing to use it with pride, I am making a political statement.

I wondered if my approach to being in relationship to the world was one of being radical, of pushing for social and political change simply by existing. I considered that maybe it wasn't the relationships themselves that were in some sort of static position that could be labeled radical, but that the choices we make in how to cultivate relationships were constantly moving towards the radical. Maybe radical relationships are ones that create a safe space in which to explore what makes you uncomfortable—things like accountability and nuance. I came to define a radical relationship as a relationship that is watered by radical values, fertilized by curiosity and warmed by the light of compassion.

As I wrestled with all of this, I realized that when talking about radical relationships, I didn't want to talk about romantic or sexual relationships exclusively. Those can of course be radical in their approaches, in many different ways. But I want this book to also offer insight and advice on embracing and fostering a radical spirit in all your relationships—with your friends, family, coworkers and fellow activists. I want to empower you to be a force for change, not by making those around you follow a prescriptive path, but by making choices that inspire those around you.

My mantra for the last few years has been "I cannot control anyone except myself." It's been a gentle reminder to surrender my knee-jerk reaction of trying to overextend myself as a way of maintaining some sort of control of what's happening around me. No matter how frustrated I may feel, telling myself that I cannot control anyone except myself is a way to take a deep breath and let go of unreasonable expectations. It is also a reminder that I cannot control anyone *except myself,* as in recognizing that I am not completely devoid of power or influence over my life, and I get to make decisions about what I do, how I do it and who I do it with. Fostering a radical relationship with myself has been one of the hardest and most important things I have learned to do.

Interestingly, as I began to work on figuring out how to have a relationship with myself based around accountability, trust, taking risks, sitting with discomfort and allowing myself to make mistakes but also encouraging myself to do a little better today than I did yesterday, it rippled out. I noticed how this approach impacted my relationships with loved ones. I set boundaries not from a place of fear and avoidance, but as a way to make the discomfort we felt into something we could both sit with and untangle together. I also saw how my self-relationship work influenced how I did activism work, encouraging fellow protesters to outline ways people could contribute that weren't all or nothing "in the streets direct action" or "writing letters to Congress." I found myself being vulnerable with my friends in a way I used to reserve only for my romantic partners and making space for them to be vulnerable with me in exchange.

While many of the examples and stories I share are about friends and family, much of the same concepts can be applied to relationships with people outside of your inner circles too. Over the last few years, I have found a lot of joy in forming casual but caring relationships with many people I interact with day-to-day. I've befriended my neighbors, which has included baking treats, helping with basic repairs and chatting about our lives. I met the person who owns the business under my apartment complex and shook their new baby's tiny hand. I regularly text with the person from the auto shop next door, with whom I share a passion for taxidermy and old Teenage

Mutant Ninja Turtle figurines. I wave and smile at the local postal worker as they go about their rounds, and I sometimes leave a labeled snack for them in my mailbox. After many years of isolation due to the pandemic and my own burnout, I have made a point of connecting in small (hopefully noninvasive!) ways.

I didn't start cultivating those relationships with any desire to see a return past maybe trusting we would help each other in a fire or an earthquake. Being in a city, my neighbors' level of preparedness in a disaster is deeply connected to my own. To some extent, we rise or fall together. Taking a small-town neighborly approach to urban living felt like a necessity, especially as I witnessed what happened in disasters such as Hurricane Helene and the wildfires in California. I didn't want to wait until we were struggling to build a safety net. Still, I have found that those little kindnesses I started doing to build a shared investment in our neighborhood continually pay me back with interest! When a drunk driver sideswiped my car at 7:30 AM, my downstairs neighbor jumped out of bed to record it and call me, while the business owner who lives across the street called the police. If they hadn't been willing to go out of their way, I may never have gotten the driver's insurance to pay for the damage. My auto mechanic neighbor helped fix my car, getting me the best possible deals on parts and labor, and since he saved me money, I paid him extra to compensate for storing the car. In a separate incident, the postal worker found out I was missing a package and went above and beyond to track it down. I have undoubtedly directly benefitted from being neighborly and investing in those around me. When our government and media encourage us to be suspicious of our neighbors, especially if we're different from each other, it is a radical act to refuse that fear.

The COVID-19 pandemic confirmed what I have long held to be true, which is that mutual aid and shared investment are powerful forces for building community trust and power. I don't know the explicit politics of the postal worker who services my apartment. I don't know who my downstairs business owner voted for. But rather than let those things define our relationships, I've gotten to know them as people and as members of my neighborhood, and they've gotten to know me. It's allowed us to be good neighbors first. This shared trust also helps open up genuine dialogue—I remember listening to the auto shop owner voice his worries about Antifa, and then mildly saying, "Oh, interesting! I've been doing street medic work with antifascists for years, here's been my experience!" Because he knew me and liked me, I was able to shift his mind a little by listening, not being dismissive and encouraging curiosity over being "right" or "winning" a debate.

Sometimes it's not just about the information, but the way you frame the message. One of my best friends, Avens, once told me that in the political work she does, she's not trying to take social advantages away from anyone (namely, those who hold many of them, such as straight white men). Rather, she wants to create a world where *everyone* has access to the resources, advantages and social grace that the most privileged have benefitted from. While I don't always agree with that framework, I do think it offers an entry point to discussing social advantages when talking with a privileged class, and this approach might get us all further than righteous anger.

As someone who is a vocal leftist, I hear a lot of people say, "It's not my job to educate." That's usually true—it isn't, and the patience required to educate others often feels like a luxury that we can't afford. I have struggled with this aspect of navigating disparity and taking action against injustice because I have learned over the years that it isn't really *anyone's* job to educate others in good faith. But all of us have room to grow, and people do still need to get that education from somewhere. I've heard "Google is free," and sure, it is, but search engine results are tweaked and influenced by the searcher's past search history, advertising and institutional biases like racism and sexism. If I tell someone to "just Google it," and they are deep in a QAnon, Trump-fueled panic spiral, they're less likely to get fact-checked, legitimately researched articles in their top search results. So, while it is not my job to be a guiding hand, it is often also in my best interest to offer some help if I want the person I'm speaking to to have good-quality information.

One of the best ways I've personally found to handle this conundrum is to try to assess if the person I'm talking to is asking questions in good faith, or if they are trying to be contentious. I look for logical fallacies in their responses, especially if the responses are hostile towards me personally. I try to figure out if they are actually looking for information, asking open-ended questions that suggest curiosity, or if they seem like they're trying to "win." Sometimes, even if I suspect they might be arguing in bad faith, I'll try to talk to them privately to better understand where they're coming from, especially if they appear to be a person who benefits from social advantages on the surface. By taking the conversation private, there is less of an incentive to be performative about outrage and less shame about acknowledging where you might have not considered a good counterpoint. I'm far more likely to get somewhere with someone arguing in good faith, who may be more open to new information, and this way, I also don't exhaust myself arguing with someone who just likes to stir the pot for the sake of it.

Similarly, if I am talking to someone who has fewer social advantages than I do (especially if they are subject to the disparity being discussed), I am a lot more likely to slow down and say, "I hadn't considered that. Can you tell me more or offer me some resources so I can educate myself further?" This helps me ground myself, so I don't speak out of turn from a defensive place and allows me to better understand how they have come to this position. It also gives me the opportunity to check their sources in my own time. I never demand it, but asking this puts a little bit of work on them to offer up some suggestions of places to start, and also communicates that I'm willing to do the labor of reading up more on the topic.

LOVE REBELS

The stories and practices I present here are ultimately about what being a love rebel has come to mean for me. It's about having firm and compassionate boundaries. It's about self-awareness and knowing how and when to ask questions of those around you. It's about short and long-term strategy and about choosing which hills are worth dying on, and which to leave to fight another day. But it's also about deciding to treat people like they're not disposable, letting them grow and evolve and change (that means yourself, too). It's about recognizing that real compassion isn't being a pushover, but rather tapping into a core strength kind of love. And it's about finding ways to be an activist with strong values without burning the candle at both ends.

I have many complex relationships in my own life, and I am still trying to find a balance between my convictions and my compassion. In the past, I have absolutely burned some bridges. Frankly, there are bridges I'd burn again just to make sure—I can be just as petty as the next person! It's fair and reasonable to have boundaries around what you can be patient about, and what you can't. Every person has to decide for themselves where the line in the sand is, and I encourage you to have one.

This is not about loving your enemy, but rather, consciously asking yourself if it's worth riding into battle against this person today. I speak to you as someone who has the scars of doing activism in a non-sustainable way and has burned out dramatically more than once. I just hit a point where I couldn't be angry all the time without it taking a serious toll on my mental and physical well-being. There are better, more sustainable ways for us to fight oppression.

Love Rebel has multiple meanings. Being a love rebel is being someone who pushes against the easy categorization of what love means and who love is for. I also like the idea of it as a suggestion—that we should perhaps love rebels by having curiosity and compassion for people who are against the status quo. Finally, it is a verb: choosing love can be inherently rebellious at its core in a world that seeks for us to separate ourselves into walled gardens. This is hard work, but I truly believe it's worthy work.

QUESTIONS

* What made you pick up this book?
* In what ways do you conduct your relationships radically?
* In what ways do you engage with politics radically?
* What does being a love rebel mean to you?
* Do you know what your lines in the sand are?
* How would you like to manifest being a love rebel in your life?

CHAPTER 2:
POWER DYNAMICS: ACKNOWLEDGING DISPARITY

I remember being on a date with a friend I knew from my queer adult content community, a hot Black butch. They prepared a lovely cheese plate and we snacked and talked about our lives over brie and figs. I don't remember how exactly we got to the topic—maybe I was ranting about police violence; I do talk about that a lot—when my date casually said, "Yeah, I remember having to explain to a white femme lover once that if we were pulled over together, I needed her to put her hands on the dashboard immediately, because if she made any missteps, I'd be the one who got shot." They just chewed thoughtfully on their cheddar and Ritz crackers while I sat there, totally taken aback. I had never even thought about this view and was rocked by the realization that this was a daily calculation for my non-white friends. It's been seared in my mind ever since, and I'm grateful for that, even as it horrifies me.

No matter how radical we may be, or wish to be, we still exist in the framework of -isms and -phobias. Racism, sexism, ableism, classism, sizeism, xenophobia, homophobia, trans-phobia—all these and more blend to make up the world's worst shit smoothie. Many types of inequality influence and mesh with each other, creating a tangled mess of uncomfortable feelings and awkward questions. When I was growing up, I often felt absolutely and desperately overwhelmed by the awareness that everything was connected. I felt so small, like no matter how much I worked and learned, how could I ever hope to make the world a better place or even begin to be a better person myself? It was so much bigger than me.

Oftentimes, when the topic of privilege and disparity is raised in conversation, especially online, it quickly becomes charged. When we feel uncomfortable, we may want to shy away from what's causing us that discomfort. We may try to avoid it by saying "This is a no-politics zone," or "Let's just agree to disagree," or something similar. I don't know about you, but I feel that that approach almost always fuels the flames even more. "Just calm down" has never worked to calm people down in my experience—it just comes off as dismissive and infuriating.

Alternatively, discussions of privilege can devolve into comparisons of who has it worse and therefore is the most correct in the conversation (as if those things are connected). Social advantages are by their very nature conditional and often vaguely defined. I live under the poverty line in my city, for example, but I also have a savings account and rent an apartment—I have untold wealth and security compared to some of my friends and to most of the world's population. I am white and cisgender, which affords me a lot of privilege in my day-to-day life. I am also fat, queer, disabled and a woman, which can complicate the advantages I receive. So, am I privileged or not?

Many folks with some form of social advantage (including me!) have subconsciously learned to be preemptively defensive when someone talks about institutional oppression, to protest that we are exceptions to the rule, that we are aware of these things but we're working on it. We usually don't intend to silence those we're talking to, but there is often an undercurrent of "I'm one of the good ones; don't you trust me? What more do you want me to do?" This response only serves to center me in the conversation, rather than meaningfully address the topic at hand. It allows me to stop feeling discomfort and start feeling smug, which is a much more comfortable feeling. Defensiveness has a silencing effect, even if that's not at the forefront of our minds. And that absolutely ripples out, impacting our relationships explicitly and implicitly.

So, how do we strike a balance between fostering spaces for growth—even and especially painful growth—while also recognizing that everyone is at a different stage in their journey? How do we keep the door open for discussion without letting in people who are more interested in hostility than reflection? How do you assess if a question is in good faith or bad faith?

I'm still figuring that out myself—I'd love to say that I have infinite patience and want to hear everyone out, but I have my limits, as do we all! But I have come up with a few techniques that have enabled me to test the waters on how invested a person is in understanding another point of view and how interested I am in understanding theirs. I've also figured out what to ask myself so I can nudge my own discomfort. Like stretching, sometimes it's painful at first but leads to long-term improvements in flexibility.

By encouraging myself to just sit in my feelings and listen more than I talk, I have found myself not only expanding my understanding of how different people experience the world, but also becoming more resilient to anxious, uncomfortable feelings. This improved resilience has served me well in that I am now more capable of answering genuine questions without it feeling too raw. While I'm not infinitely patient (nor do I think that's an ideal to strive for), I am a lot more patient than I was even five years ago. My ability to hold that space and to explain things that may be hard for someone else to understand has enabled me to be in more active allyship with marginalized people, so they don't have to do the labor all the time. Working on myself allowed me to be better at helping others work on themselves.

None of us will ever be perfect. I say that I'm not an expert on consent culture or activism or social justice work because I am in a constant state of learning and unlearning, scraping away at layers of assumptions and assimilation that have calcified over the years. But rather than finding that scary, I now find that exciting and freeing. How wonderful to be in a position of constant learning, to be ever able to do a little better tomorrow than I did today! How fulfilling to continually add to my ability to relieve suffering in others through compassionate action!

ATTITUDE ISN'T EVERYTHING, BUT IT HELPS

It also helps to consider and redefine where my ethics are, a constant process as I take in new information and discard old ways of seeing the world. Hammering out what my beliefs are—both what I feel certain of and what I'm still defining—helps me clarify what my intentions and goals are when having this kind of introspection and helps me to be more alert to the ways disparity shows up in day-to-day life. Am I trying to reflect on institutional racism so I can be a better friend and advocate for my Black neighbors when they're struggling with our landlord, for example? Am I learning about animal welfare and overcrowded animal shelters so I can speak up for the unhoused community when talking to the city about housing projects providing space for pets? What do I plan to do with the education I am pursuing to better support people who are already doing this work or experiencing these injustices every day?

I try to educate myself on an array of topics, from the cryptic and arbitrary rules around gender testing in sports to the long-term effects of electric cars on the environment. But for many of these topics, I am not seeking to inform policy or lobby my local officials; I'm mostly just engaging in arguments on social media. I want to be informed, certainly, but I choose my battles and educate myself far more on the issues for which I'll be engaging in direct action. Most importantly, it helps to be humble about what I know and what I don't know—being honest about that allows me to hear what other people are saying and to be open to new information without defensiveness.

Awareness is of course a vital and important first step to navigating and understanding the power disparities in our relationships, but it's only the first part. Action is also important, and manifests in many different ways. Conscious action can appear in how we talk about power disparities with others and in how we acknowledge and resolve conflict. We might see it in the kind of direct actions for which we step forward in leadership and the ones for which we step back. Even when we recognize our own physical responses when we are feeling defensive, slowing down so we can take a deep breath and remind ourselves that we are not under attack—all of these are important next steps to taking our awareness and making it into something tangible.

One of the most important things I have done to improve my relationships with others, educate myself on perspectives I don't share and take a much-needed step away from a rescuer mentality, was to quietly and consistently participate in activism groups where I was the minority. By showing up and listening more than I talk, I strive to decenter myself and my identity in the activism I participate in. I learn a lot this way! By being a helping pair of hands, a financial donor or a street medic, I am able to offer myself as a resource while also witnessing the human experiences of the people around me, many of whom are very different from me in myriad ways. It also serves to remind me that no identity is a monolith—no one will agree with someone else one hundred percent of the time on tactics or end goals. Different gay people have different definitions of liberation compared to one another, as do different Black folks from each other, as do different people with disabilities. Exposing yourself to a diversity of opinions helps to expand your understanding of the issues while offering practical assistance to and being guided by the people who are most impacted by said issues.

NAVIGATING DISPARITY

I'm writing this book while watching the rise of authoritarianism, nationalism and xenophobia around the world. I live in the United States, where the institutional attacks on the most marginalized groups of people have been steadily increasing, but it's not just happening here. I have friends who remain horrified that Brexit passed—meaning that the United Kingdom left the European Union—which was due in part to class division and anti-immigrant rhetoric. Far-right parties are increasing their power in Canada. I have other friends who are trying to help evacuate people in Ukraine, Sudan and Gaza. Academics who study the decline of democracies and how that leads to a rise in fascism have been increasingly sounding the alarm. We are seeing alienated white people being attracted to and invigorated by the false promises of white supremacy, usually spurred by fear of their own loss of power and privilege. When that fear collides with leaders who are willing to appoint a scapegoat, we have historically seen mass atrocities. We are seeing those atrocities now, too.

Young white people sometimes express frustration that they feel they can't do anything right or are expected to hate themselves. White people in positions of power and influence often tell other white people to assert themselves by shutting out other perspectives instead of listening to and learning from marginalized communities. Folks with social advantages encourage each other to mock and scorn those without. Rather than finding compassion and solidarity, we see people increasingly willing to throw others under the bus if it means grasping, however tenuously, to some privilege that might help them get ahead.

Due to all this, I've been thinking a lot about navigating disparity. It can feel really difficult to know what to do or how to act, especially as different marginalized groups express disparate and sometimes contradictory pleas for action (and especially when those actions are equally valid responses to injustice). I am constantly made aware that the world we live in is a complex and often paradoxical place, where nuance is everywhere and simple answers are rare. I encounter a lot of loudly stated demands that people should behave in a certain way, failing which they are implicitly supporting all kinds of horrific actions, from genocide to transphobic violence to authoritarian theocracy. But, as I said earlier, I try to remind myself that I can only control my own actions and behavior, and therefore I focus my work on expressing my choices and being open about how I come to them, rather than telling other people what they must do.

I want to encourage critical thinking and allowing for nuance. One of the best ways to push back against cruelty and bigotry is to be able to analyze what's happening and why, what words people say and also what they leave unsaid. Understanding power imbalances and disparity can be a useful tool for listening fully to people who are being harmed. That understanding is also helpful when we're trying to find compassion for people who are scared and in finding compassion for people who are lashing out. That doesn't mean enabling them or forgiving them, but understanding the context can make our work to counteract them more effective. When we become comfortable acknowledging disparity, it gives us space to analyze what has happened, from both an individual and a more social perspective, and helps us figure out what to do about it so it doesn't happen again.

QUESTIONS

* What are some ways you are marginalized in your day-to-day life?
* What are some social advantages you have?
* What is a situation where you noticed a power imbalance that benefitted you?
  ◉ Did you acknowledge and address it, and if so, how?
* What is a situation where you noticed a power imbalance in your life that had a negative impact on you?
  ◉ Did you feel safe bringing it up?
  ◉ Why or why not?

CHAPTER 3:
SELF-CARE CAN BE MUTUAL AID

Content warning: this chapter discusses suicidal ideations and self-harm.

Activism is hard work and the need for it never ends. Whether you're talking about ethics with your therapist or at school, helping run a soup kitchen or educating yourself on the history of injustice by reading books or watching documentaries, it can be a lot, and it can overwhelm you very quickly. I can't count the number of times I've called my parents sobbing that all the causes I care about are connected, which makes me feel like whatever I do, it is never enough. There's so much to do, and I have bounced wildly between feeling grimly determined to take it all on and feeling like I'm being buried under the pressure of it all.

It took me many years, a lot of therapy, the right medication and an active, ongoing mindfulness practice to get to the place I am today, which is calmer and more resilient. I spent my teens and twenties feeling anxious and depressed all the time. I had regular nightmares about what would happen if I had an opportunity to do good and I didn't take it. My anxiety manifested in an array of nervous behaviors: picking my skin, biting my nails and engaging in substance abuse and self-harm. I was looked at as a community leader, which made me feel like I was doing something positive, but privately I was an absolute mess. I was also extremely anxiously attached in my relationships. I wasn't eating consistently or well. I dealt with daily harassment and threats from online trolls and neo-Nazis. I felt like I was constantly being observed, so I had to put up a facade of being strong and driven while internally I felt like I was going crazy.

I attempted suicide more than once. That led me to get a diagnosis of depression, and I started taking medication for it. Many years of burnout went by before I had an epiphany: I didn't want to die because I felt there was no hope. I wanted to die because I just wanted to rest. I didn't know any other way of stepping back, because taking a break felt like complicity.

Part of the issue was that I didn't feel like activism was something I did—being an activist was something I simply *was*, in the core of my being. I didn't feel like I could say no to anything related to fighting social wrongs. In a world with so many terrible things happening, how dare I want to take a moment to breathe? What a luxury to even have that as an option! Radical self-reliance is the goal, right? I interpreted this as meaning it was weak and needy of me to lean on others. I needed to toughen up and get my shit together, I scolded myself. I regularly punished myself for even thinking about how this was impacting my well-being, and I pressed on.

It almost completely broke me. I was more than burned out—I was smoldering ash.

I had a full and public emotional breakdown in 2012, and it was honestly really embarrassing for me. My friends went to Reddit to try and track me down because they were afraid that I was going to die from suicide, and they were right to be worried. I didn't realize then that I was screaming for help. I also didn't realize how much I was scaring the people who loved me. I really did feel like my only option was to jump into the void of the hereafter just so I could breathe.

What changed my mind about giving up? Much of the change happened over time, as I began to reach a greater, more holistic understanding about what exactly I was feeling and where it was coming from. I started seeing a psychiatrist who didn't think I was actually depressed, but rather that I was suffering from undiagnosed ADHD (which was destroying my ability to focus or plan ahead) and general anxiety disorder (which made me feel like I was doomed). I stepped back from identifying as an activist 24/7 and from seeing my value as entirely wrapped up in being in service to others. I changed my focus from "fixing things" to "acting in solidarity with others," and reminded myself that whole communities exist doing any kind of work I can think of, and it's not a burden I need to struggle with alone. One heroic dose of DMT—a particularly strong psychedelic—made me absolutely convinced I had died in my friend's backyard and that I had shat my raccoon onesie, (which was emotionally fine with me, though I felt a little pity for my friends who would have to clean up the mess). Waking up the day after, I felt spooked at how sure I was that I had died the night before. And that's when I realized that I was not ready to die yet. Suddenly, all the work I had been doing to understand my headspace crystallized for me—I wasn't suicidal when I felt overwhelmingly *sad* but when I felt overwhelmingly *desperate*. Knowing that helped me figure out tools that were more effective at keeping me in balance. Rather than trying to focus on whether I was happy or sad, I began to focus on whether I felt supported or alone.

That clarity reframed another major pattern that I recognized in the community around me: the number of friends and acquaintances who were dying. So many of them were fierce advocates for the marginalized and destitute, and yet they felt hopeless and alone. Despite how invested they were in their communities, they didn't feel safe asking for resources and support for themselves. They were dying from suicide, from overdoses, from physically and emotionally taxing themselves past the point of sustainability. Radical self-reliance can have a devastating cost.

I began to try to understand how this was happening by looking at individual social media posts, the pages of public activists and how the media talked about activism. I noticed how many community leaders would do everything in their power to help other people but were embarrassed to ask for support for themselves. I noticed how many communities relied on mutual aid networks for things like feeding those in need or offering harm reduction workshops and I also noticed how the media often demonized those same networks as "hostile" and "antisocial," judging the people involved for their multicolored hair and black clothes instead of finding out what they were actually doing. While no one should do activism for the clout, it does weigh on you when the work you do goes completely unrecognized, or, worse, is treated as harmful by the world at large. But was that the whole story?

None of this fully gelled in my mind until early 2024, when I became a mentor to an evangelical teen. As part of my self-education to understand the culture this teen was raised in so I could better support them, I began to read evangelical material and stories from people who had left more problematic sects of the Church (often called "deconstructing"). These stories repeated refrains such as "I felt scared," "I felt scared of going to Hell," "I felt scared of what people at my Church would think," "I felt scared I wasn't a good enough person." People in this situation felt constantly doomed, like they needed to be performing "goodness" and "faith" 100% of the time, and even then, they might still burn in Hell forever. Nothing was ever enough.

Learning about "religious scrupulosity" really changed how I related to the feelings of anxiety and guilt this teen mentee shared with me. A type of obsessive-compulsive disorder, religious scrupulosity can manifest in many ways: invasive thoughts about Hell, a need to repeatedly repent or confess, constantly second-guessing your actions and thoughts or combing through past words and deeds for things that may upset God or your Church. It sounded a lot like the behaviors and thought patterns I was hearing about from my evangelical mentee. And that yawning hungry pit of despair sounded familiar to me. It's how I felt about activism.

It turns out that there is also moral scrupulosity outside of religion, where you may obsess about "good" vs. "bad" actions past the point of useful reflection. You might excessively worry that a past action was immoral and what people might think if you were "found out." You might pointedly avoid situations or conversations addressing moral ambiguity. You might repeatedly seek reassurance about the nature of your thoughts or actions, going over various hypothetical situations to "test" your moral response for the "right" answer. You might punish yourself as penance for not doing enough or obsess over how people perceive you. While it's important to reflect on our intentions and actions, there comes a point where it's no longer healthy or useful, but that can be hard to recognize when you're in it.

In short, there are people who feel they must be hypervigilant against the manifestation of "the sins of the world." Some are taught to feel that way thanks to how some pastors preach about the Bible (like in religious scrupulosity). Others learn this quiet underlying dread by observing the way activist infighting manifests online (like in moral scrupulosity). There are also folks who go the opposite direction—people who are strangely serene and just don't engage in self-criticism or feel anxious. These people may be so indoctrinated that they disassociate from critical thinking, choosing to avoid anything that makes them feel uncomfortable or challenges their beliefs. I will admit that for a while I hated them, but I also envied them.

As an atheist who was raised Pagan by pretty chill parents, I can't really speak with authority on what causes that sense of guilt when it comes to religion. But I can speak to my own experience of realizing that I was sometimes using language as an avoidant excuse, treating the phrase "self-care" like a get out of jail free card that allowed me to sidestep challenging myself in any way. I also felt guilty when I saw that behavior pattern in myself, which would cause me to scold myself into working harder and being more judgmental of myself rather than figuring out how to find balance and how to make activism feel less like a constant slog. Even while working on this book, I had to check in with myself and ask whether I was taking up a new hobby instead of working on the book as a form of self-care or as avoidance. Did I genuinely need to rest (a valid need!) or was I just dawdling because the work felt too hard?

This is a battle that I am still wrestling with on an ongoing basis, especially the more I read from marginalized writers like Roxanne Gay, Kai Cheng Thom and Julia Serano. As a white, cisgender woman, I am advantaged enough that I could ignore a lot of people's struggles if I chose to do so. And as a disabled, queer, fat woman, it would also be easy to focus exclusively on struggles that impact me personally. Choosing not to ignore suffering I don't experience has been a large part of my radicalization and how I show up for my community. Finding a balance between doing that and taking care of myself—making sure I get enough rest, eat properly, engage in things that bring me joy—is part of how I show up for myself. Finding direct actions that I can do offline is also part of how I show up for myself. Taking care of others is good for my heart and being in community is good for my spirit.

I have struggled with both believing that yes, we need to put on our oxygen masks first, while also being very frustrated at how many people just do that and never bother checking if anyone around them needs help putting theirs on. Sure, we need roses as well as bread, but roses won't fill your stomach! As hard as I've tried to acknowledge that self-care is important, I have also found myself burned out when my fellow activists opted out of following through on a community commitment, leaving me to pick up the slack (which cut into my own self-care time). Due to those kinds of experiences, I certainly feel frustrated when I feel like the people who could more easily stand up to oppression choose instead to seek gratification (importantly, not rest) at the expense of solidarity. I'm still pondering this and trying to make sense of it.

I think it's important context to recognize that the concept of rest as resistance comes from Black performance artist and activist Tricia Hersey, who was writing to other Black folks about rest as a way of disrupting and pushing back against capitalism and white supremacy. Her book *Rest is Resistance: A Manifesto* is about how truly resting is not about filling an empty cup to then pour out for others (thus keeping even rest as part of a cycle of recovery to work more), but to break the cup entirely and rest for the sake of rest itself. My understanding of the concept is that it's not a white Instagram influencer wellness trend or an alternative to showing up for struggles against oppression, but rather a way for marginalized people to complement their struggles in the world.

As a person with some privilege and some marginalizations, I think my personal embrace of this balance is still in its infancy. I will say, though, that I've learned the hard way that no matter how hard I grind, I can't dismantle abusive institutions by myself. For me, it has felt important to find ways to weave self-care moments into my day-to-day life, not instead of direct action, but as a supplement to it. I learned that I don't have to give up my life for a cause, but I personally can spare a few hours a week or a hundred dollars a month to help others fight injustice without cutting into my need for rest for the sake of resting. I also acknowledge that I am lucky to be able to do so. I decided that I don't have to be perfect every day, but I do want to be a little better today than I was yesterday and that's an achievable goal for me. It's better for my mental health to do a small amount sustainably and slowly build my resilience by asking for help when I need it than to do too much and then curl into a fetal position and completely avoid activism as a whole because I am totally burned out.

If we want to be in a position to offer solidarity from a place of strength, we need to make sure we take care of ourselves. As a bonus, sometimes volunteering for an hour at the animal shelter will boost your mood, get you out of your head and be healing in ways you didn't expect. When you aren't overwhelming yourself, you may be more capable of adaptation, which makes you a more centered member of your community and harder to knock off kilter. Self-care is mutual aid, and mutual aid is self-care. Each informs the other.

WHAT IS SELF-CARE?

Self-care, of course, is easier said than done. What does it look like? How can I tell if I'm recharging my battery or if I'm shirking my responsibilities? Well, I guess it's one of those things that you constantly have to be in conversation with your mind, body and spirit about, checking in not as a form of judgment but as a gentle practice of accountability. What looks like fucking around to one person is another person's deeply meaningful meditation. For example, while working on this book, sometimes I stepped away and baked a cake or watched a few episodes of a fun TV show. Choosing what you consume in your down time is also important—I have books on my reading list that are emotionally intense and intellectually provocative, and I have graphic novels that are just candy for my brain. Both are super important but each has a different role!

I once had a lover who told me that "You make time for what you care about." He said it to me as a mantra, a way of reminding himself (and me) that the intention of what we *want* to be spending time on or what we think we *should* be spending time on is not as informative or useful as what we are *actually* spending time on. I often say it to myself as a way of being in the moment when I feel overwhelmed. What am I filling my day with, and does it serve me or my goals?

I ask myself this not as a way of invoking a sense of guilt, but rather to investigate if I need to reprioritize to represent my goals of the moment better. By asking myself this, I've discovered not only daily habits that keep me from being my most productive, but also daily habits that really encourage me to blossom! For example, I am happiest and most calm when I take the time to make myself a filling and balanced home-cooked meal. It gives me a space to be creative and I feel better physically when I am eating properly. It also pushes me to get up and move around. As a writer, it's all too easy to get lost in sitting in one place for many hours, but then I eat junk that gives me gut issues instead of food that nourishes me, my hips get tight and I struggle to sleep soundly and my head aches because I'm staring at a screen. Cooking two solid meals a day breaks up my workflow in a way that makes me better at writing, and it's become something I look forward to instead of something I dread.

Another example is how I set up working on this book. I have ADHD, and for many years, I would procrastinate on projects until the last minute, then charge through overnight. I produced acceptable work, but I spent a long time feeling bad and putting myself down for not doing what I was "supposed" to do and then letting my anxiety drive my work in a panic. I wasn't enjoying my "self-care," and the way I was implementing it led me to feel manic, not centered!

So, I broke up the book into sections I figured I could write 1000–2000 words on, figured out how many days it would take for me to do that, gave myself weekends off and scheduled daily writing time. It's been a way more enjoyable and creatively satisfying experience when I set myself time to be both on and off the clock. It gives me a regular, easy-to-achieve daily practice but also allows me flexibility for days when I just don't feel like staying indoors and writing. I can see progress, which makes me feel less stressed. I can comfortably enjoy time with friends when I'm not in my work hours. And, because I'm not completely exhausted, I feel more capable of being in touch with my muse when I'm at my computer.

I also allow myself a lot of grace, to be honest. I didn't always—in the past I would try to motivate myself through scolding and punishment, and it just didn't work. It made me more avoidant. I've noticed myself occasionally falling into a pattern where my self-care manifests as me using one task I need to do to procrastinate on another task I need to do. Bouncing from one to the other allows me to feel like I'm getting away with something while also getting all of my responsibilities taken care of! Last week I didn't want to sit in front of my laptop, so I went to the laundromat, got myself a coffee and hung out with a friend while the washer was running. That recharged my battery, so when I got home, I procrastinated folding my laundry by working on a chapter of the book. Then I procrastinated on making dinner by folding my laundry. Having different things that I could do in small chunks gave me a chance to change up my day, from sitting to standing, from creative thinking to repetitive motion. This ended up being a system that appealed to my ADHD need for novelty while also checking things off my to-do list. It felt great!

Here are some things I have learned about having a healthy relationship with yourself while also being an activist:

Good Boundaries

When I am in the flow, I put my phone on Do Not Disturb, put on some motivational music (I personally really like lo-fi for concentration) and set a timer for myself. This is a way to establish boundaries with the outside world and its demands for my attention. It's a boundary on my mind with a musical cue that "now is for work," and a boundary on my time, so I don't end up sitting in front of the computer staring at a blinking cursor.

I like to work forty-five minutes on, fifteen minutes off, so when I'm writing I'll set a timer, or if I'm folding laundry I'll listen to a fun podcast. When the podcast is over or the timer dings, it's time to get up, stretch and do something else for fifteen minutes. And when I've come to a good stopping place with my writing, if it's over a thousand words, I'll step away and be done for the day. Good boundaries make good neighbors, and that's true for any demand on your time, including self-inflicted demands. When people around you trust that you have good boundaries, that allows them to trust the ways you show up that little bit more because they know that your "yes" means something.

Keep Up Momentum, but Pace Yourself

It's really tempting to set our goals high and push ourselves hard. Work hard, play hard, right? But I found that when that was my strategy, I ended up working too hard and not having any energy to play hard, or play at all. Then I would feel reluctant to get to work the next day because I'd still feel tired from the day before, so I would treat myself. The next thing I knew, I had been playing the Sims for hours and it was too late to work on the book. Whoops.

Now, I have found a strategy that allows me to work at a consistent pace. I step away before I feel frustrated and exhausted, which helps me feel excited to get back to it the next day. I give myself structured time off to putter in my garden or hang out with friends or read. I step away from the fun activities before I feel overwhelmed by them, too. It's often better to show up for 30 minutes a day for a week than to do two hours all at once and then feel drained and unwilling to show up again. Pacing yourself is not only self-care, but also community care. When you demonstrate that you're someone reliable in the ways you work, people can count on you in a way that leaves both of you feeling good, not resentful.

Pleasure is Revolutionary

"If I can't dance, I don't want your revolution." "We must have bread and roses." These are two phrases (with a number of variations) that I see a lot in leftist communities, intending to demonstrate that it's important to have a balance between survival and thriving. They were an influence on me as a young woman navigating the world of activism. But I want to refer to the full quotes of both because I think they communicate something even more important:

> What the woman who labors wants is the right to live, not simply exist—the right to life as the rich woman has the right to life, and the sun and music and art. You have nothing that the humblest worker has not a right to have also. The worker must have bread, but she must have roses, too.
> —Rose Schneiderman, June 1912 speech

> At the dances I was one of the most untiring and gayest. One evening a cousin of Sasha, a young boy, took me aside. With a grave face, as if he were about to announce the death of a dear comrade, he whispered to me that it did not behoove an agitator to dance. Certainly not with such reckless abandon, anyway. It was undignified for one who was on the way to become a force in the anarchist movement. My frivolity would only hurt the Cause. I grew furious at the impudent interference of the boy. I told him to mind his own business. I was tired of having the Cause constantly thrown into my face. I did not believe that a Cause which stood for a beautiful ideal, for anarchism, for release and freedom from

```
convention and prejudice, should demand
the denial of life and joy. I insisted
that our Cause could not expect me to
become a nun and that the movement
would not be turned into a cloister.
If it meant that, I did not want it.
—Emma Goldman, Living My Life, 1931
```

What strikes me about both of these quotes is that they are indeed saying that pleasure is important. But they are also saying that *pleasure itself is inherently revolutionary.* It's just as much a part of what we're fighting for as the necessities. Pleasure isn't something that only the privileged should get to have.

Activism isn't always a party, and doesn't need to be. Sometimes the work is hard and gritty and tiring and still needs doing. But I think sometimes we forget as activists that it's just as important to cultivate our joy, to have some fun together and to remind ourselves of our "beautiful ideal." We must not only think about what we are fighting *against* but what we are fighting *for.* I suspect that finding an equilibrium between labor and pleasure is what nurtures us and makes activism sustainable in the long term.

QUESTIONS

* What are some methods of self-care you have found especially centering in your life?
* What fills your cup?
* Is there an example of something you used to do as part of your self-care routine that doesn't serve you anymore?

* How do you balance taking care of
  yourself with activism right now?
    ◉ What would you like to improve?
    ◉ Where do you think you're getting it right?
* What are some ways you can make more
  room for pleasure and ease in your life?
    ◉ How about in your community?

PART TWO:
GET PERSONAL

CHAPTER 4:
RADICAL FAMILIES (AND THEIR FEUDS)

If there's one thing that the *Fast & Furious* franchise has taught me, it's that family is everything. Family can mean a lot of different things: from blood family, to adopted family, to close friends who are basically family. Family can change, too (though, while I appreciate how often protagonist Dom Toretto turns his antagonists into collaborators and eventually "family," I would exercise far more caution in the real world.) Personally, if asked to define my current family, I would list my father, my half-brother and his direct family, members of a family I grew up closely with, a couple of best friends and the roommate I've lived with for the last five years. I get along with some of them more easily than others, and we do not always share political beliefs, but there is a shared investment both emotional and practical that leads us to put in extra effort to understand each other.

I was very lucky to grow up with parents who not only had political leanings close to my own but who were also very supportive of my work and activism. I believe that when I decided being in the streets was important, the lack of tension at home did a lot to bolster my resilience and determination from an early age. I knew that if I was arrested, my parents would have my back because they believed in fostering my compassion even when there were consequences. I know that I am blessed to have that kind of support from my closest family, even when other members of my family disagree with my beliefs or strategies.

Experience doing direct action with my blood family and navigating how to find common ground when our action plans differ has been an incredibly useful core around which to build a strong, loving, productive framework with my chosen family. Learning how to forge forward with activism in an equitable way, how to disagree without escalating unnecessarily and how to let a loved one have autonomy in how they show up have all been vital skills when navigating these things with a friend or a romantic partner. Understanding the ripple effects that certain kinds of activism can have on the people around us, directly and indirectly, has also helped me talk transparently with people I live and work with about what actions I'm drawn to and how that might affect them. Being willing to discuss what activism I am driven towards and acknowledge the potential impact on those around me—finding ways for us to give informed consent before the fact as much as possible—has been a necessary form of compromise I was lucky to practice with my parents first.

We learn some of our most core ethics and patterns from our families, whether we manifest those ourselves or rebel against them. One of the values that was passed down to me was making sure to share the load when it came to doing work, whether it was housework or activism. We didn't believe in gendered labor in my house, so it was kind of a shock when I started organizing with other people and began to notice how often women were doing the cooking, cleaning and notetaking at meetings, while men did a lot of the pontificating and proposing of actions. This experience influenced how I organize my own actions and how I participate. I ask people what roles they want to be doing and find a way to strategize around that, with any unwanted jobs that *must* be done traded around so everyone takes a turn. You want your activism buddies to be enthusiastic and driven, not resentful and withdrawn!

One quote I've seen passed around on social media is, "Sure, he's well versed in leftist theory, but does he wash the dishes?" I think that speaks to the way people talk "as activists," but then that praxis sometimes falls away when they're at home. With that in mind, aim to make sure that your type of activism doesn't rely too heavily or disproportionately on labor that is historically shoved onto disenfranchised people (like the dishes are often pushed on women, even in the most punk co-ops I've encountered). It's something I've noticed about accountability circles, for example. Accountability circles are a process of restorative justice, wherein someone who has done harm is given an opportunity to recognize that harm and engage in a process of making amends to the person harmed and the community as a whole. These circles in practice are often made up of people who are not cis men who are banding together for the accountability of a cis man (usually a white cis man). On the surface that may not seem like a big deal, but in practice, it puts a lot of work on the shoulders of people who likely struggle with having their boundaries crossed by institutions (such as the medical profession or their workplace) all the time for the benefit of someone who systematically benefits from said culture of boundary crossing. Try to mix things up so that any labor is evenly spread, and make sure to give people breaks if they need to step away to recharge.

The work I do around consent has caused me to consider what the ripple effect of my actions might be. For example, being at protests as a street medic raises the possibility that I might answer the door to a cop looking to pump me for information, something that's important to talk about with anyone that I live with. My online activism has led to me being harassed by alt-right message board zealots, something which is mostly contained to the internet, but that can increase the risk of a SWAT team being called to my house to scare me or white supremacists looking for where I live so they can attack me.

When you are an activist, particularly one who is doing activism some consider subversive, it comes with attached risks. Therefore, it's really important to talk to those who will be impacted by that risk about what they feel comfortable with. If you live with dependents or others who may be extra impacted, that should be something to take into consideration as well. For example, if you are a white middle-aged person and armed police break your door down because of an angry post you made online, it might scare you, but it could traumatize a child or be a deadly situation for a Black person. Taking a moment to weigh the risks and benefits is just good policy. It may not mean that you never perform an action that makes the people around you uncomfortable, but at least you'll be inclined to think about the consequences and give them a heads up. Sometimes, you may decide it's not worth the trouble, and that's OK.

Particularly in the United States, we are told that everyone is an island and that nothing we do should affect others. It's just not true. We are people, not islands, and the consequences of our actions ricochet around us in ways we can't always predict. What *is* important, at least to me, is that people do *something* to support those who are more marginalized. It's too easy to opt out from participating in activism in any tangible way when you benefit from the systems in power, but that inaction becomes complacency when democracy is at risk and authoritarianism is on the rise. When we think about how we can show up, it's sensible to consider the needs and tolerance levels of those around us in case the shit hits the fan—that way, you'll have a crisis plan to fall back on, you won't have to worry about your loved ones talking to the police and so on. It's also the ethical thing to do. There are many ways to contribute to activism and you don't have to choose the most dangerous options to be doing something powerful! Encouraging people to turn up, to feel a little discomfort as a way of increasing resilience and demonstrating solidarity with people whose lives are politicized and who can't opt out, is terribly necessary. But it doesn't mean you have to go chant on the streets, either.

This leads me to some thoughts about things you can do with your family and loved ones, whether they want to support a protest or participate in the community in other ways. I have a mental process I go through when I'm trying to figure out what I want to do and how I want to plug in, which I go into detail about in the next part of the book. It boils down to figuring out what I care about, what I'm good at and who needs that right now, and then finding a pace that allows me to follow through sustainably. You can use this process for yourself and with your family. Whether your family members are older or younger, there are lots of ways to engage them in your activism or to join them in theirs for an issue you all believe in.

If you have family members who want to go to a protest with you, there are several strategies I would keep in the front of my mind: knowing each other's red flags, working at the risk level of the least comfortable, communicating effectively and keeping an eye on your family. Go at their pace, both emotionally and physically, so that you can take care of each other in a sustained way. I offer more in-depth explanations of what that looks like in practice in Part Three, where I discuss how to get involved.

I really love talking to people a generation or several older than me about the activism they did growing up. I learn a lot from listening! It's great to hear about strategies that worked or didn't work, how activism made them feel, if they felt their work ended up meaning something or felt hopeless and much more. I find that asking questions and being curious about their experiences can make me feel validated in some of my own experiences. And sometimes, talking to people younger than me about issues in age-appropriate ways helps me better explain why these issues exist, and what we can do to push back. Explaining to a child why I put a brick in the back of my toilet as a form of water conservation reminded me how important it is to do something tangible, even if it's ultimately a drop in the bucket.

Learning how to share my activism with my family, both blood and not, helped me figure out what really mattered to me, how to pace myself so I didn't burn out entirely, how to ask for and receive help and other skills that have made me more effective as an activist. Sharing has also helped me learn how to value all different kinds of contributions, to meet people where they were rather than trying to push them into being what I wanted and made me more responsive to struggles that came up in the process. I feel like I learned a lot about letting go of a specific outcome and instead value any step forward, no matter how small.

All of this advice is good if your family shares some activism that overlaps with you, but what do you do if that isn't the case? What should you do if your grandparents constantly want to talk about the moral imperative to ban abortion and you're pro-choice? Or if your cousin is a Zionist and you're passionate about a free Palestine? Or if your sister was at the January 6,

2021 riot at the Capitol and you're an anarchist organizer? How do you move forward if you cannot do so together?

In the last ten years of a divided populace in the United States, it's felt increasingly impossible to talk to people with different beliefs. It can feel like everyone knows their position is the correct one and wants to win you over to their side. You might find yourself with this tendency too, of wanting to argue because with enough logic they *must* be persuaded, right?

One of the things I've had to learn, for my own peace, is that many people reach the ethical positions they hold not through logic, but through gut feeling. Their beliefs feel right even if the data doesn't always support them. Given enough time, money and determination, you can find a study to support all kinds of misinformation or an article that will bolster any theory. If a person doesn't trust a group of officials to give them accurate information, no amount of arguing about it with citations will change their mind.

Case in point: there is a band that I've grown to love called the Insane Clown Posse (ICP), with two white, Detroit-based lead rappers who dress up as black-and-white painted horror clowns and rap about camp levels of gore and violence. They are often referred to as "the world's most hated band," and are constantly the butt of jokes, censorship and even prosecution (famously, the FBI had their fans—Juggalos—flagged as a gang). Well, there's a line in what is maybe ICP's most famous and most taunted song, *Miracles*:

```
I don't wanna talk to a scientist
Y'all motherfuckers lying,
and getting me pissed
```

The media had a field day with this statement, laughing at these two grown men dressed as clowns who refuse to listen to science about how magnets work. And I get it—on the face of it, it looks like a pair of high school dropouts refusing to even try to understand how science works and choosing willful ignorance. It can feel really frustrating!

But then I started to really think about it. Do *I* know how magnets work? Like, really know? I had a vague idea, but it was a lot more complicated than I would have initially thought. Listening to lectures by scientists in the field, I realized how inaccessible the language and concepts they use to communicate often are to the average person. A gulf lies between academia and the people, and it isn't entirely the fault of the people that the gulf exists, even if the scientists never intended for such a barrier to exist.

Maybe this disparity is not so important when it comes to the intricacies of magnets—at least not day to day—but we learned during the COVID-19 pandemic how vital it is to explain scientific data in a humble and easy-to-understand way. We saw how various governments handled and mishandled a global health crisis when it came to their explanations about how infectious disease spreads. Bridging that gap in science communication can and does mean life or death. In an effort to help with this issue, I read all the studies and statistics I could get my hands on so I could better break it down for the people around me. Even as someone with higher education and who has learned how to absorb this level of information, I didn't find this straightforward. There was just so much information, and some of it contradicted other information. I began to understand why someone might not want to talk to a scientist and why they might feel lied to and angry about information coming from the scientific community or government—information that they didn't understand.

Some of the people in my community have topics they feel so strongly about that they cannot and will not communicate with folks who are on the other side of the argument. Honestly, it isn't always worth maintaining those relationships, especially if it comes at a cost to you. I find it very difficult to talk to or even listen to people who believe that all fat people are fat due to a lack of willpower, for example. And if someone refuses to treat me with respect or acknowledge my humanity? Staying in contact with them may well be more trouble than it's worth. I am not so confident in my abilities to believe I can change every mind!

It is absolutely OK to pick which hills you're willing to die on—if any—and to stick to your guns with those issues. You don't have to be individually responsible for the education of everyone around you. It may be instrumental to your mental health and safety to distance yourself from people who believe differently from you, especially if that belief involves dehumanizing you or your loved ones. That is a choice you get to make for yourself. Good boundaries make for good relationships, up to and including cutting people off.

It's also very possible to have strong, healthy boundaries that embrace some distance and include the ability to say certain topics are off-limits without cutting people off entirely. What's really useful in my experience is setting clear lines for what is and is not OK, writing them down for later reference, and being consistent about the enforcement of those lines. I had a relative who found it difficult not to make comments about my weight because she struggled with and felt bad about her own weight. I told her that the topic of my weight was off limits for her and that if she insisted on bringing it up after being reminded, I would leave her home, wait a month, and try again. This made it very clear what behavior wasn't OK, what I would do about it if it happened, and a timeframe for whether I would return. It was really hard to keep enforcing that boundary, but by having a script for myself, I found it easier not to get angry in the moment, but just clearly and politely remind her of the rule and then follow through with distance if she didn't stick to it. Eventually, she got the message and stopped bringing it up, and our visits were much more pleasant.

I would have had every right to just cut her off for repeatedly crossing a clear boundary. For me, I considered how important it was for me to have a relationship with this relative, our different generations, the communication norms we were raised with and how much her comments would impact me. I decided after weighing those things that I valued her and was invested in her enough to stick it out and see if we could redirect that energy. I accepted that I did not have control over her behavior, but only over how I responded to it. Only I could make the assessment of whether it was "worth it" for myself, and by handling it in this way, I felt I had agency in our interactions without feeling like I was banging my head into a brick wall.

Part of the reason I chose to do this is because of the work I do in consent culture. I've learned that people grow up with many stories, and their families and communities tell these stories repeatedly until they believe them. Sometimes people aren't even conscious of their bias until someone points it out to them. Unpacking systemic oppression, stereotypes and disinformation can take a very long time. It can feel extremely scary and unmooring to disentangle the things we "know," and while it isn't my responsibility to educate others I sometimes wonder, if I don't, who will?

This comes up in particular when it comes to organized religions, cultlike groups, conspiracy theorists and other groups that care more for obedience than critical thinking. It can feel tempting to distance yourself from people who are engaging in cultlike behavior patterns, and distancing may well be the right choice. If you need to do that for your safety and the safety of those around you, temporarily or permanently, that is of course absolutely fine! It is not your responsibility to be a lifeline to pull people out of the dark. I cannot be invested in every person I come across, so I limit my focus to people whose well-being I care deeply about. Sometimes you really can't do anything to help, and while that's very hard, you may find yourself needing to make peace with it.

That said, a lot of research indicates that the most effective deprogramming technique is not using force, cajoling, threats or shutting people out. What *is* effective is holding space, gently and with firm, compassionate boundaries, where you can continue to communicate and strengthen ties. Many high-control groups rely on isolating their members from any other community, which increases the group's influence and grip. I remember when I learned about how many door-to-door missionaries are prepped to expect hostility from the people whose doors they knock on, further underlining that people outside of the high-control group will never welcome them. When that proves to be true, it pushes them further into the arms of the church. This mindset really changed how I engaged with Jehovah's Witnesses—by talking with them from a place of cheerful curiosity instead of annoyance, I found they were also curious about my lifestyle and the calm I exuded. Instead of conflict, we learned something from each other, building off of things we have in common (a desire to help our community, for example) rather than focusing on the ways we differ.

By continuing to connect with your loved one, you are providing a much-needed example of another way to live. By not pressuring a person to live in the same way as you, but instead letting your actions be the testimony of your ethics and beliefs, you can provide perspective without preaching. I have found that when someone holds strong beliefs that I believe are erroneous, no amount of logic and facts are going to dissuade them, as logic and facts often pale next to feelings when a person has a troubled heart. Being patient, asking open-ended questions and genuinely being curious about the answers, sidestepping away from the things we fiercely disagree on and instead talking about the things we share—all of these things have enabled me to hold space without being attached to an outcome. Sometimes I'll tentatively ask questions like "Huh, that's quite a statistic! I'd love to look into that more. Can you tell me where that comes from?" This allows me to chip away at misinformation indirectly. And, I hope, if they are open to knowing more, this approach allows them to feel safe bringing their doubts to me without me judging them.

Boundaries and picking your battles can be the difference between feeling like a husk of a person and being able to have connections with people you disagree with but can connect to on other levels. Again, only you can ultimately decide if a connection is worth the effort. As long as it's safe to do so, I would gently suggest trying to make sure you're extending the same grace to others that you want for your own mis-understandings of how the world works. I won't say that no human is disposable—there are outliers for everything—but I think many humans are less disposable than we treat them. Separating behavior from the inherent being of the person can help us decide to invest or to divest.

QUESTIONS

* Which members of your family have you felt comfortable talking about politics with, if any?
* What types of community mutual aid or other activism could you come together with family members on?

* Do you have family members with whom activism
  or politics have been a point of tension?
    ◉ Can you think of some creative ways
      you could work together on a proj-
      ect that you can all agree on?
    ◉ In the case of family members who are not
      attuned with your viewpoints, what are some
      healthy boundaries you could outline and enforce
      when they push back against your activism?

CHAPTER 5:
SAILING THE USS OWNERSHIP

Even with the most radically inclined family (chosen and oth-erwise), there are times when things have shitty consequences, no matter how careful we think we're being. One of the most difficult things I've experienced in being a radical activist and trying to be in a radical relationship with the world is when I just...fuck up. And it happens all the time! Sometimes, I say something poorly and it ends up unintentionally hurting someone. Sometimes, I am more committed to serving my ego than I am to serving the cause or the community. And, I'll be honest, sometimes I have meant to hurt someone because I felt righteous about it at the time. It's taken a lot of time (and a lot of therapy) to be able to be humble about my own wrongdoings. There is also a lot of freedom when you learn how to take ownership gracefully.

It's painful to admit when we've crossed a line. It's often scary to acknowledge. We live in a society that pushes dichot-omies in all things—you are good or bad, right or wrong, innocent or guilty, abuser or abused. To acknowledge that we've caused harm can feel terrifying, like we're saying that we're a horrible person, past any saving or redemption. I hope that you know that I'm not someone who takes that approach at this point in the book, but I do understand where it comes from.

Even as a consent educator, it took me years to keep myself from immediately getting defensive when someone told me I hurt them. The thoughts that would swirl in my head were panicked ones: "I've been misunderstood! I'm a good person. I would never do that! At least, I would never intend to do that... Well, OK, maybe it happened, but it's their fault really!" Defensiveness is a natural self-protective response, sometimes from a place of shame, sometimes from a place of fear, sometimes from a place of hurt. And yet, just because it's a natural response doesn't mean it's a healthy or helpful one. While I understand my impulse to yell, "Are you for real right now?" when a bag of potatoes slides out of my pantry onto the floor, the potatoes aren't doing it *to* me. It just is.

At some point, I decided that I wanted to put more effort into understanding why I was acting defensively and what I could do instead that would be more productive. I began to shift my own internal narrative about receiving feedback from, "They're saying this because they hate me. What a punishment!" to "They're saying this because they trust I care and want to do better. What a gift!" Rather than assuming that feedback, from criticism to a callout, was the opening shot in a boxing match with a winner and a loser, I chose to see it as an invitation to collaborate together on a situation that could be improved. We could both be winners. Just changing that mental framework vastly reduced my anxiety and my lack of defensiveness de-escalated most conflicts that might have otherwise arisen.

When someone tells me I hurt them, I still feel the anxiety pang in my stomach and the flush in my cheeks of shame, but now I can stop myself. I've learned coping mechanisms to sit with my immediate discomfort, practicing some mindful breathing and grounding, listening more than I talk and gently nudging those defensive thoughts to the side with a reminder that I'm not under attack. I can tell myself that this information will help me to improve so I'm not crossing boundaries and causing harm, and that it's wonderful to have such feedback.

Later, once I've heard what the person has to say and I've thanked them, I can reflect on the situation further. That's when I can consider the context in which the feedback was given, my history with that person and if I can see where they were coming from. Sometimes, I genuinely can't, or I think the critique is unfair or out of proportion. Not all feedback is given in good faith, and not all community members are invested in shared growth! Sometimes, a "callout" is intended as retribution. However, if I don't react defensively—if I choose to react as if it is being given in good faith and receive it as such—it will empower a person who really is hurt and will disempower someone trying to get a reaction out of me. Either way, the result is better than a defensive response would have gotten.

Genuine accountability and restitution are themes I tend to gravitate towards in my writing. I think that these are concepts we are often taught to be afraid of, rather than curious about. Learning how to give a genuine and thorough apology is a useful skill, and one we don't really learn. Growing up, I was often told simply to say sorry. Maybe if I was particularly petulant, I would be reminded to "say sorry like you mean it." But different people appreciate different kinds of apologies. Some people want to hear the acknowledgment that you feel regret about the impact of your actions. Some want to hear you take responsibility for the impact of your actions and acknowledge that what happened was not OK. Still others want to hear what you'll do in the future to ensure it doesn't happen again, and what you will commit to in order to fix the harm done. And some folks really want to be asked for forgiveness. Knowing what the person reporting the boundary crossing wants to see from you will help you better assess what you can offer them. Personally, unless otherwise informed, my approach is to acknowledge what I did wrong, what I should have done instead and what I'll do better next time, which I think covers the main bases and allows for some action points the person can hold me to.

Sometimes, the situation can't be resolved quickly and I just have to sit with the fact that someone is hurt and needs to be in that space for the time being. That's certainly hard, especially as a recovering people pleaser, but I have found it vital to remind myself that to try and push them to feel better is to take their agency away from them, which only compounds the issue. Learning to sit with someone's discomfort without trying to fix it on their behalf is an important skill, not only for situations where I am taking ownership but more generally. My rate of burnout has gone way down since I stopped trying to anticipate the needs of everyone around me and instead learned to trust that they would tell me what they wanted me to know when they were ready.

The secondary effect of this kind of introspection and mindfulness is that it models for others a different way to be when it comes to conflict. I think that we often expect people to either flare up back at us or to be openly dismissive, and both are upsetting and often inflammatory. By instead reminding our anxious brain that the only person we can control is ourselves, we can focus on the things we can do and worry less about the things we can't. And by showing that we're taking feedback seriously and using it to be a little better today than we were yesterday, people feel less tense telling us when we fuck up, because they feel more confident they can trust that not only will we hear them out, *but we actively want to.*

Of course, this isn't foolproof. There will be times when people will accuse you of harm because they want to make themselves look more powerful by tearing you down or because they want to retaliate for some slight. Here's what I've learned from years of being a leftist on the internet: just the simple change of not reacting defensively has effectively de-escalated most potential online conflicts. By having aggressive good faith in others and staying measured in my reactions, I have been able to learn how to be a better member of my community. And I've witnessed other people be inspired by my approach and then mirror it in their own lives. There is a sense of relief when you no longer fear accountability but welcome it.

What if it's not you being held accountable, but a loved one? It can be challenging to support someone without being defensive and protective on their behalf. Even without being the center of attention, figuring out how to acknowledge your feelings about the criticism requires space and patience. You might feel confused, angry, hurt, betrayed. You might question your experiences of your loved one, picking through memories for red flags, or you might feel like the community is against you, too.

I'm a consent educator and I have gotten this wrong, even while trying to do everything right. A partner of mine was called out for violating boundaries, and I went through stages of reaction to it. I initially felt taken aback and suspicious of my partner and her intentions. Then, as we talked, I trusted her recounting of events and turned against those coming out with the callout (wary that they were more invested in punishment than growth). As I gained more information, I lost trust again in my partner's story, which culminated in her withdrawing and me leaving her. Years later, when I saw her talking about how I failed to hold her accountable for her boundary violations, I was shocked, hurt and deeply angry. I don't know how much

I could have done differently with the information I had then, but I know that I should have recused myself from acting as any kind of mediator. So, I want to say first and foremost—even as someone who is a semi-professional around these issues—this shit is hard! It's OK to find it difficult.

Let's say someone you're close to—a friend, a lover, a family member—is called out on social media. Someone makes an accusation against them, and it spreads throughout your social circle. Just like when you're the subject of the callout, you should start from a place of taking a step back and breathing. When this has happened to me, I have felt a rush of anxiety grip my stomach. I often want to demand more information. I want to lash out at something I feel blindsided by or I might want to be a character witness. All of these things come from a real place of caring for your loved one, but they are all counterproductive. These knee-jerk responses almost always make the situation worse and leave everyone involved feeling more upset.

Instead, encourage your loved one to take a break from social media for a couple of days. Consider taking one with them. The criticism will still be there once you've both had a chance to breathe and ground yourselves. If they feel they must say something, I recommend starting from a place of humility. For example, using phrasing like "I have seen this, and it's given me a lot to reflect on. I'm going to take (a specific amount of time) away from social media to think about this/talk to my therapist/consider what next steps I can take to be accountable, and I will return and speak on this (in this way at this time)." This is helpful in de-escalating the situation because it demonstrates that they are invested in reflecting on what has been said, getting professional advice and speaking to the community about what they plan to do moving forward. This technique also makes it clear that they will be addressing the topic soon, after taking some time to do some soul-searching, with a date that others can hold them to. That helps the people making the callout feel seen and heard without a fight.

This period of reflection and introspection is a good time to brush up on community accountability practices. The United States is pretty reliant on the carceral system as the main way of "seeking justice." That said, the communities I'm a part of know damn well that the system was not built for us and our loved ones—the more marginalized we are, the less likely we'll be able to afford justice through police and courts, never mind handling the racial and classist assumptions that govern the prison industrial complex. Thankfully, that isn't the only way to seek accountability and solutions, it's just the one that we've been spoon-fed.

There is a lot of excellent reading available to help explore and construct some sort of transformative justice model, and when at all possible, I recommend starting to broach those discussions before someone is in the middle of a callout. What does your community think about these models? Have they tried them before? What interests them about transformative justice, and what makes them wary of it? Do they think it can be productive and effective? By having these conversations as theory rather than trying to solve an immediate problem, you can make them a little less scary.

These conversations can be a lot of work, mentally and emotionally, and can bring up feelings and assumptions we haven't really thought about before, such as trust in the law, who "deserves" punishment, who "deserves" mercy and so on. If you're already feeling charged because someone you care about is being held accountable, it will increase the difficulty level. As the loved one of someone in the middle of this, I would encourage you to look into what resources are out there and make use of them as applicable. The references section at the back of the book is a good starting place, but I would also suggest looking into what community mediation resources might exist in your circles. I know in the Bay Area, where I live, there are a couple of nonprofits that help mediate conflict as a neutral third party, from personal issues to landlord/tenant disputes. If such a thing exists near you, that may be something you can suggest your loved one offer to the people who feel harmed.

I also think it's really helpful, as a person in allyship with the subject of the callout, to read through any text that outlines the issue if that exists (often called receipts) and try to pull out what the actionable points are. Does it spell out specific harms? Is there a pattern of behavior? Is there a possibility of a misunderstanding here that might need clearing up? With your knowledge of the parties involved, do you think that your loved one made a misstep and acted against their own values, or do you think their ethics are just not the same as the ethics of the person calling them out? Does your loved one recognize the situation being discussed and do they agree that they made a mistake? Helping the person you care about through this process of reflection compassionately but responsibly can help resolve it.

When I've been called out, it has been invaluable to have people around me who I trust to care about me enough to educate me when I need it, and to also (metaphorically) kick my ass if I dig my heels in. Being able to rely on people I know are invested in me ensures that I can take in feedback, helps me feel less anxious and enables me to focus on what I can do to be a little better today than I was yesterday.

It's also really useful to help the people we love understand that there is often (though not always) a difference between "being an abuser" and "doing abusive behaviors." I know in the circles I run in, the two are typically used interchangeably.

Moreover, I think our society actively rewards us for engaging in abusive behaviors as a way to survive an incredibly fucked up world. We don't culturally value mental health. We value getting on with it and shutting off our pain, so yeah, that's sometimes gonna bubble up in awful ways. Sometimes, it's gonna harm us, sometimes, it's gonna harm other people. I have grown to believe that the lack of separation between "abuser" as an identity and "abusive" as a behavior descriptor does our society a disservice. I suspect it makes it easier to distance ourselves from the ways we (or those we care about) engage in boundary-crossing behaviors, from a little pushy to abusive. "My friend/partner/family member can't be an abuser!" we say. "They don't fit the profile!" If we spell out the behaviors themselves, however, out of the context of people we know, it often becomes easier to say that the person crossed a boundary inappropriately.

When we tell someone we care about that their behaviors caused harm, whether it was a mistake or intentional, whether it was thoughtless or abusive (or both), we can also say to them, "I don't think you want to cause harm, so how can we work together so you can acknowledge the impact of your behavior and make a plan for what you will do differently next time." It says to them, "I trust you didn't want this to happen, and I'm here for you as you do the introspection that will help ensure it doesn't happen again." Rather than being a way to avoid accountability, focusing on abusive behaviors insists on more accountability—they are not inherently an abuser, they are choosing to engage in these behaviors, and they can choose not to. This strategy reassures that person that I do not plan to abandon them while also making it clear that I am not going to enable being shitty either.

None of this is to say that abusers do not exist. They absolutely do! I think they're a lot rarer than social media would have you believe, however. Part of the reason I am a big fan of community coming together to gently and firmly encourage ownership and growth, instead of kicking people out, is that kicking people out usually just means they continue to cause harm elsewhere, whether out of malice or ignorance. I'd rather at least try to help them acknowledge and learn. If they refuse, then I can put up my walls knowing I tried, and they weren't ready or willing.

Transformative justice often feels like a lot more work than more toxic approaches like police and lawyers or getting into a public morality debate. In some ways, it can be. To help hold someone accountable from a place of love and growth means you need to have some intense discussions and it can be uncomfortable. That's why I think it's so powerful to do a lot of strategy conversation and discuss values when strengthening the community, so that we have each other's backs, even when we fuck up and especially when we disagree with each other. It's because of my solid community and our shared investment that I'm a lot more able to bring someone who has fucked up closer, to talk about issues openly and to come up with an accountability plan that is healthy and doable, rather than either ignoring the issue and washing my hands of it as "not my circus," or banishing someone from the community to "keep the peace."

As I said earlier, I really don't believe that most people are disposable. I'm open to the possibility that some people really are awful and don't bring anything to the table, but they're few and far between. I think we dispose of people because the idea of being a part of an accountability process sounds exhausting and we're already stretched thin. That's valid! But that's also why I think it's so important to get others involved: other mutual friends invested in compassionate ownership, professional mediators, activists with experience in these processes. I have learned that in the long run, mediations are less emotionally taxing than constantly being paranoid that people are talking behind your back or secretly dislike you, or feeling like you have to contact anyone who is connected with the person who messed up to make sure they know what happened. In practice, those kinds of more avoidant "account-ability processes" often end up being more harmful and less productive, so I don't use them unless the pros absolutely outweigh the cons.

The painful fact is that as much as many communities claim to be radical, they are still often intent on narratives of punishment and binaries. It's difficult to reimagine what justice might look like in an alternate future where we are deeply invested in each other's evolution. Because of that, you may do many things that feel ethically "right," and some people may still be furious at you. You may try hard to be impartial, but another person may say you're being too soft because you care about a person. There may even be a grain of truth to that. You also get to decide where your boundaries are and what your ethics guide you to do, not only as a support to your loved one, but as a member of the wider community. Sometimes there is no tidy resolution and you may have to leave a community or take space from the person you care about while they work on their shit. Only you get to decide where you draw the line.

Mutual care is part of being in a community, as is mutual accountability and mutual responsibility. Being there for each other includes moments when we need to establish with someone we care about that they crossed a line and that it wasn't OK. Learning how to hold others accountable with the grace we also want them to extend to us in turn is an ongoing and constant process, and I learn more about it every day. But one thing I feel pretty sure of is that I want to live in a world where people aren't scared to say they have been harmed, and where people aren't scared to take genuine and heartfelt ownership for the results of that harm. By helping the people we love to feel like accountability is an expression of care and an opportunity to do better, we can cut down on the defensiveness that all too often multiplies the initial harm. "Be the change you want to see" can sometimes be as small and yet as powerful as holding those close to us in love and accountability. And that fierce care—for our boundaries, for our loved one's growth, for our community's trust—ripples out in ways we may never fully recognize.

QUESTIONS

* Think back to a time someone told you that you hurt them. How did you react?
  * Why do you think you reacted that way?
  * How would you like to react if it happened today?
* Have you had an experience where someone you cared about needed to be accountable for harm?
  * Did you speak to them about it? Why or why not?
  * Would you do anything differently now?

PART THREE:
GET
INVOLVED

CHAPTER 6:
WHERE DO WE START?

If the world were merely seductive,
that would be easy. If it were
merely challenging, that would be no
problem. But I arise in the morning
torn between a desire to improve the
world and a desire to enjoy the world.
This makes it hard to plan the day.
—E.B. White

When it feels like everything is on fire, how do you choose where to start fighting back? This is a question I get a lot and it's a question I wrestle with often, because I think being an activist means figuring out where to start over and over again. It can be overwhelming when you think about all of the intersections between injustices and marginalizations; how can you possibly choose when everything is related to everything else? With so many ways to begin untangling the answer to this question, I figured I would walk through a very brief, very simplified version of my own current activism action plan to give you an example of how you might embody this for your own work.

I identify strongly as an antifascist. Now, this is a big and somewhat amorphous identity that can splinter down into lots of different directions with different approaches. Personally, while I care about the creep of fascism in various manifestations, I also know that to try and fight it on every front will lead to me in a fetal position rocking back and forth. Therefore, the first thing I use to narrow my own approach is ask myself what my personal skill set is. I know that I am good at teaching people how to de-escalate conflict, I have basic street medic skills, I write compelling essays, I can make TikToks and I'm experienced in constructing codes of conduct/backend logistics for grassroots organizations. I also know that some things are not my strong suit: intense physical labor, tech/ operational security, being a fundraiser host, being available on a regularly scheduled basis and other things. This assessment is impersonal and doesn't have a value judgment attached—I just know that I am a lot more available to teach a once-in-a-while workshop or to write a piece when I feel called to than I am to make it to a weekly meeting.

With that in mind, I'll consider my personal causes. I care about LGBTQ+ rights, I care about anti-racism, I care about addiction, I care about homelessness. That's not to say I don't care about other things, of course, but that I go further out of my way to take action on these topics. I'll also roll around in my head what my special interests are, my hobbies and my areas of nerdy curiosity. For example, I am especially interested in the spread of infectious diseases, the history of the working class, cooking, gardening, crocheting and tabletop role-playing games. These may not immediately sound relevant to real-life issues, but bear with me! The last thing I'll think about is what groups and resources already exist in my community, both my physical location and my emotional communities, like my friendships, my family and my online circles. Where can I pitch in? What could I utilize and network?

Putting all of this together, I can begin to flesh out a few ideas:

* I could teach a workshop on de-escalating conflict for marginalized people who want to avoid calling the police at a co-op community space or café.
* I could write an essay introducing people to lesser-known antifascist activists in history, playfully suggesting how to "get their look" by sharing some simple activism tips related to their work and listing resources for more information.
* I could organize a beginner's one-shot tabletop game for unhoused folks with the help of a local outreach group.
* I could put together a TikTok post on the importance of needle exchange programs and link to some harm reduction programs.

All of these ideas include me bringing together something I'm good at, something I'm interested in and a way to connect groups of people. Sometimes it's focused on something fun, and sometimes it's focused on something practical. Sometimes I can do the item all by myself, without any help from someone else and sometimes, it encourages collaboration with a group. Any of these could be put together without a lot of financial support and in a short timeframe. They are also one-time things, so they don't have an ongoing commitment that I might struggle with. None of them are exclusively antifascist—they intersect with other issues—but all of them are relevant to the antifascist cause. All I have to do now is look at my calendar and chat with organizations or venues as appropriate to see if what I've come up with would be a good fit for them.

When figuring out what kind of activism you want to do, I recommend starting small and building from there. It's so much more powerful (and sustainable) to show up consistently and to be reliable than to offer too much of yourself and then need to take a long time out of service recovering. Whatever your availability and interest, there is a way you can lend a hand to your cause! The hardest thing to do is to cross the threshold and get started, but it really is about putting one foot in front of the other. It's about doing *something*, not doing *everything*. And don't forget, it's just as important to encourage community through just having fun together. I love to volunteer at the library to read Halloween stories to kids or with an animal shelter or to host a board game night at a community center. These kinds of community outreach are not only important for filling our cup with joyous experiences, they also often allow us to meet and get to know people from multiple generations and life experiences, which widens our scope.

I can't stress enough, however, that just because many things could use another set of hands, you don't have to be doing everything every waking moment. In fact, that's a sure-fire way to burn out! While none of us are free until we're all free, and all these things are connected, it's OK to specialize, especially if you make sure to follow the lead of people who are doing other types of activism that you aren't as involved in or informed about. To offer an example, I make an effort to watch media produced by Black and brown folks, read books about civil rights and the ongoing fight for racial justice and pay Black and brown artists for their poetry, paintings and music. I keep reading and learning about how to better be in solidarity with Black and brown folks while recognizing that I will never be as tuned into the issue of racism as the Black and brown folks who live it. So, I listen to their requests for support, and I help where I can in the ways I am asked to serve. Learning what you don't know is an ongoing process and one that I find interesting and engaging.

There is something meaningful in showing up for those around you without it being accompanied by "a cause" or a protest. I appreciate this statement, which I first read from Mia McKenzie of *Black Girl Dangerous*: "I will no longer use the term 'ally' to describe anyone. Instead, I'll use the phrase 'currently operating in solidarity with.'" I think there is something really powerful to this reframing, where being an ally isn't about declaring yourself as such and then resting on your laurels, but consciously choosing to act in solidarity with others. A lot of this kind of activist work, like speaking up when someone makes a racist joke at work or correcting a person who misgenders someone isn't showy or exciting; it's the daily, quiet activism that keeps society evolving towards something more equitable for all. People pay attention to what we do when we aren't drawing attention to ourselves.

You might also find yourself drawn to a certain approach or group simply through proximity, and that's also fantastic! Your workplace might have a union you can get involved in, for example, or your religious community might do a soup kitchen or a clothes drive you can help out with. You might be more inclined to do something more logistical and bureaucratic, like join a board at a local nonprofit or take notes at a town meeting. Or that might make your skin crawl, and you would prefer something like helping an artist collective create a mural to beautify the local park or organizing a nature walk to teach people about the local flora and fauna. Whether you create an activist opportunity from whole cloth or plug into one that's connected to your day-to-day life, whether you have a lot of experience or none, many paths are available to find your footing as an activist.

On that note, asking for help is one of the most radical things I have learned to do, and is probably the most important activism I model day-to-day. But it's hard. When I am close to burnout, I really struggle to name what may be helpful. I know I want or need help, but I'm not sure what asking for help exactly looks like and my brain is mushy so I can't think of anything offhand to ask for. Similarly, when a well-meaning person has offered help, I have struggled to name what I'd actually appreciate. This isn't just something that happens to activists—in fact, I usually experience this when someone else is having an emotional breakdown, recovering from a medical issue or dealing with grief. If you are a person for whom that scenario feels familiar, check out the resources, where I have listed a bunch of different types of help you can ask for or volunteer to provide. The list is just a starting place, but I've found that having specific things I can point to in my exhausted state and say, "This please!" has helped me ask for what I need or offer something I am able to give.

While protests themselves are an important part of activism, they are just one strategy of many. I want to recognize that people who go and do direct actions are able to do so often because of a strong network of unseen people doing all kinds of support without ever being at a protest. If your heart is with that kind of activism, there are so many things you can do, both to support an action as it happens or to foster community care and civic involvement to strengthen those vital ties! I have certainly known people who felt that they weren't doing anything significant for "The Cause" but they were preparing food, helping with household tasks, offering a safe container to complain, and even taking protesters on day trips to help them decompress. When you do these kinds of care support actions for activists who are doing emotionally and physically risky actions, you are doing the invaluable work of taking things off their plate so they can maintain a healthier rhythm. That's a key component for making these strategies effective.

I can't stress enough that sustainable activism, on or off the street, means being aware of and humble about your limitations. I pushed myself too hard one summer and it caused me physical pain I'm still recovering from. Remember the first rule of street medics: don't create another injury! I know it sounds trite to say you can't pour from an empty cup, but it's true. Self-care is community care, and community care is self-care, like an ouroboros of mutual aid. Pace yourself and be a role model for others by demonstrating that activism is about offering a hand. It does not (and should not!) demand martyrdom to be effective.

QUESTIONS

* What are some ways you feel drawn to "plug in" to your community as an activist?
* Have you tried a type of activism that didn't work for you?
  ◉ Why do you think it wasn't a good fit?
  ◉ What is a better fit?
* What strategies or resources could you put in place to make it feel sustainable to be more engaged in your community?
  ◉ What are a couple of things you can do to lay that groundwork for yourself?

CHAPTER 7:
PROTEST ON THE STREETS

Going out and pounding the pavement at a protest is a uniquely exhilarating and exhausting experience. Often, a public protest is one where people show up in person to bring awareness to a cause. Sometimes, you may rally in one strategic location (such as outside a city hall or a police station) or you might march in the streets, bringing part of a city to a standstill as a form of protest and direct action. Protests may be organized by a grassroots group, a nonprofit, a marginalized community or by university students. Protests are often the domain of a group who feel they are pushing against the status quo of people in power, though whether or not that is an accurate assessment is often up for debate.[4]

What makes a protest "successful"? It depends on the goals of the action. Some protests consider the number of

---

4   The 2017 Women's March, a worldwide protest the day after Donald Trump's first inauguration, is an example of a protest that encountered some friction around whose voices were centered.

participants to be the deciding factor. Others would say that it's about whether or not the protest was able to remain peaceful (and, to further break that down, "peaceful" might refer to the behavior of the protesters themselves, or the protesters *and* the police). Media coverage might be the difference between a "successful" protest or not, or the end results might be the gauge—did anything change, in the short or long term? Sometimes the goal of a protest is to prevent someone from being platformed and sharing their objectionable ideas to a larger audience, and so the measure of success is whether or not they were deplatformed. I have been to a variety of protests I would consider successful, and they have ranged all over the map in terms of goals and ripple effects.

Due to this variety, going to a protest can lead to a huge variety of experiences, only some of which you have control over. And that can be really stressful! One of the biggest pressure tests I've experienced with my relationships—romantic, platonic, familial—has been in relation to out-in-the-streets protests. However good your mindfulness practice is, being in a setting that can be emotionally and physically exhausting, startling, risky and dangerous can be a major challenge. Add to that physical discomfort and human needs (like food, water and rest) and you have a situation ripe for flaring tempers and explosions of conflict.

When you want to attend an action, it's important to plan ahead, if at all possible, especially if you have day-to-day responsibilities you need to balance as well. A peaceful protest can become violent quickly and unexpectedly, especially if the police decide to shut it down by any means necessary. You may plan on going to a march for an hour, but then find yourself kettled—a practice where the police prevent protesters from leaving an area until they are arrested or released—for much longer than you planned. Having an idea of who you'll call and what you'll do if something happens, such as if you end up arrested and held overnight or you're detained by police for a few hours, will help you feel more in control. This will not only improve your own ability to stay stabilized in a chaotic situation, it will also help you stay calm when talking to your community as it's happening.

There are a lot of things to be aware of when it comes to protests, and I'm not personally an expert on operational security (like when or how to use mobile phones at a protest). Nor am I an advanced street medic. I'm a person who goes to protests with basic first aid and de-escalation training to help prevent injury, but I haven't had to stop the bleed on a serious wound. Both of those areas are important enough that I would recommend doing some research and reading from people who have informed things to say on the matter—see the resources at the back of the book for some ideas.

What I primarily want to talk about is how to emotionally manage the intense experience of a protest so that you can stay centered and support your community, loved ones and yourself. As I talked about in the last chapter, self-care is community care and vice versa. Or, as my street medic trainer put it, "Don't create another injury." I think this not only holds true for keeping your head during an action but also when it comes to disagreeing with leadership or the crowd on the fly in regard to what direction the action will take. For example, if the march is going to an area of town with small minority-owned businesses and you are concerned about the fury of the crowd leading to smashed windows, it may be a good time to walk away. Knowing when to stand your ground in solidarity with the people you're protesting alongside and when it's time to leave is important. Remember: you cannot control anyone except yourself, but you do control yourself! Here, I'm aiming to give you some things to anticipate so you can go into these situations somewhat prepared.

BEFORE THE PROTEST

Before you take to the streets, there are a few things to think about, for yourself, for anyone you're buddying up with at the protest and for people who are your security net during and after the protest. How long do you expect to be out there? Are you dressed for the weather getting warmer or cooler? Are you wearing good socks and shoes for multiple miles of walking? Do you have enough water? How about protein bars or other snacks in case it goes longer than you expect?

I much prefer to go to actions with buddies. Ideally, I'll go with one to five other people, who I will be paying attention to and working alongside. I like to sit down with my protest buddies (sometimes lovers, sometimes friends, sometimes comrades) and talk about what our goals for the protest are. Are we trying to be in the front and hold the line against counter-protesters or the police? Are we hoping to try to place ourselves in the middle of the action to more easily get to people as medics? Do we want to march and hold signs? Do we want to paste up protest posters? Are we going to protect small businesses from the chaos? What are we, as a unit, planning to do?

Talking about this ahead of time helps create a mission statement for this particular protest so that we're less likely to argue about tactics on the ground. Just because people were comfortable with one kind of action for the environmental protest does not mean they want to do the same thing at the reproductive rights protest! I always defer to the least comfortable person I will be buddied with. You want to do everything you can to ensure informed consent and avoid coercion in the moment. It's easy to be swept up in a protest and to lose sight of your initial goals. "Talking it through as a crew," to quote the TV show *Our Flag Means Death*, helps keep us working together in harmony.

In addition to talking about our goals and intentions, I like to talk to my protest buddies about logistics. This includes red flags that suggest something may be wrong, risk awareness for the event in question and safety issues like histories of trauma or mobility concerns. For example, when I worked as a street medic for protests that were going to happen in a single space, like a park or a city center, part of our strategy was to find a place we could block off with bodies and use that as a staging area. As someone with mobility issues, this makes it a lot easier for me to participate productively. We had to be flexible (sometimes I needed to go to the person in need), but it meant that I was able to care for folks much more sustainably, and I was easier to find in the chaos.

I also know that I'm a person who disassociates in a crisis, which makes me calm during an action, but I have a bit of a breakdown a day or so afterward. Knowing this about myself means I can reach out to the extended community to find a couple of people who can check up on my emotional and physical well-being after the event. I don't have to advocate as much for myself when in a traumatized state because I set something up when I was clear-headed. It's also important to strategize for police interaction—are you willing to be arrested? If that happens, will you miss work/feeding a pet/a doctor's appointment? A certain amount of planning can help you stay calm and make better decisions rather than panicking. This is another area where I recommend sticking to the level of the least comfortable person you're buddying with. If I'm protesting with X and X needs to go to work the next day, then I will do everything in my power to make sure we don't get arrested, up to and including leaving a protest when it gets hairy.

Another aspect of this is recognizing that not all people have the same risk at a protest. Black folks, immigrants, trans people, people with disabilities—there are many subgroups of people for whom clashing with the police or, say, white supremacist wannabe militias can be especially fraught. If you are a person who benefits from social advantage in this way, be mindful and be responsive to the needs and concerns of the most marginalized in your buddy system. If I decide to do something impassioned, like throw a bottle at a cop, there's a high likelihood that the cop is going to beat and arrest my Black comrade before they beat me. We need to remember this kind of context so that we act in solidarity with each other.

It's also really important to make sure you are all on the same wavelength around security measures. When I go to protests, I tend to have a burner phone on me, though I keep it locked with a PIN to make it a little harder for the police to access my information (in the United States, police need a warrant to get your PIN, but they don't currently need one in order to unlock your phone with your face or fingerprint). I don't tend to bring my personal phone, for security and identification reasons but also because I like my phone and I don't want it to get broken! In order to make sure that my security measures are useful, I need to ensure that the people I'm communicating with also keep their phones pretty locked down, with encrypted messages for additional protection. While that's the risk balance I prefer, some people would rather be without a phone at all (understandable, they are inherently a security weak spot). I don't tend to dress in all black at protests—I choose to wear something that stands out in a crowd, like pastels. It makes me a little more of a target for the police because I won't be fading into a group, but I find the optics of punching a person in pastels tends to be unappealing to men who are trying to feel powerful, and in that way, it works well as an additional security measure. If my crew is more concerned with anonymity, it can make it a little harder to keep track of each other. That's OK, but make sure you've made that choice together in advance.

DURING THE PROTEST

OK, you've had your chat ahead of time, you have a strategy for what you're going to do at the protest, what to do if you're about to get arrested and when you're going to leave. Now you're there, and it's loud and crowded. Emotions are high. How can you take care of yourself and your protest companions in these chaotic circumstances?

While the advice that follows is through the lens of preparing for "worst possible scenarios," I also want to underline that in years of protests, I have rarely witnessed true chaos. In my experience, conflict-heavy protests against people like the Proud Boys (a neo-fascist extremist group) or the police (who feel empowered to assert dominance over protesters through the use of violence) has led to clashes between groups, but such skirmishes are typically clearly defined—antifascists versus Proud Boys and militias, or protesters versus police—and are usually avoidable. Also, I have been exasperated when the media downplays hostile instigation by the cops while getting frantic over a lone trash can on fire, writing things like "the city is in flames." Just because I talk about some things to consider when attending a protest doesn't mean they're likely or inevitable. I think it is helpful to keep your head on a swivel and to be prepared for a range of possible scenarios, so you aren't on your back foot if they happen. An ounce of prevention is worth a pound of cure!

First off, I like to pick a spot where my group can rally if we get separated or if there's an emergency. A statue, a storefront, something recognizable and preferably something that can be seen from afar over people's heads. If it's a little bit away from the street, even better. Communicate that to each other so that if someone loses their buddy, they know where to meet up with them again, even if their phones aren't working.

I also like to do a quick vibe check. Are people singing? Chanting? Do they have items that might be used as weapons? What are people wearing? Having an idea of who the organizers are and being mindful of their goals for the protest, helps me stay in solidarity while also helping me gauge if the vibe is shifting to something I am less interested in supporting. What about the "other side"? Are the cops already here? Are there folks (usually on the far-right side of a conflict) that look like "volunteer militias" or other violent groups? Are people throwing objects? Do I see smashed windows or other signs of past scuffles? Also, are members of the National Lawyers Guild (or local equivalent) visible? If so, that helps me feel confident that if arrests do happen, we have support (I write their number on my arm in Sharpie just in case). Taking a quick scan helps me get a feel for how the other participants (on both sides) are feeling. I don't mind being at protests where people are angry, and as a medic, I'm often around situations where violence is a possibility, but by getting a temperature check, I can better prepare myself for how long I am likely to want to stay, whether this is going to be a peaceful protest or if someone is likely to escalate it and what kinds of personal risk might be in play. This can also change somewhat quickly, especially as people get tired and hungry. As things get tetchier, I tend to situate myself closer to an exit point.

It's also recommended to keep an eye on the police, if they're there. Are they standing around looking casual? Do they have their shields up? Are they assembling along certain streets? By keeping an eye on the cops, I am better able to ensure that if I want to leave, I can. I also prefer to keep some distance between myself and the police, so I have more time to adjust to their behavior. And, of course, never speak to the cops!

If you will be going to protests a lot, I recommend taking some de-escalation and self-defense classes, so you have a skillset to fall back on if things get hairy. Personally, I only plan to do de-escalation at a protest with my direct buddies (and only if we've discussed it ahead of time), but I have occasionally managed to do it with counter-protesters to get them to walk away from a tense situation. I've seen someone try to tell another protester not to smash a window or burn a flag, and it escalated anger rather than de-escalated it! In the past, I have carried a big portable speaker and played songs with a chorus that's easy to join in with—I find that tends to calm people down and refocus their energy. I have also put myself between two people getting in each other's faces and loudly said to the person on the "opposite" side of me, "Hey now, let's chill out." This has worked for me between antifascists and right-wingers, and between protesters and police. It is especially effective when I am wearing those pastels. Both parties can be annoyed with me, but they tend to find someone else to fight with. Granted, this is risky! I know the risk and I choose to do it, especially as it is less risky for me, a white cis woman in "feminine" clothes. For people who are more marginalized and are more likely to be seen as inherently "dangerous," this may be too risky. It's really important to get some training so you are giving informed consent to whatever your practice is.

Finally, make sure to bring snacks, some sucking candy, gum, water and electrolyte powder. You'd be amazed how many arguments between protesters get resolved when everyone takes a deep breath and realizes they're just hungry or thirsty! Being able to share sealed food or a drink can really improve the vibe at a protest. When I feel myself flaring up, I try to remember to H.A.L.T.: am I Hungry (or Thirsty), Angry, Lonely or Tired? Maybe I am too angry to be productive here and I should step away before I create a problem for other protesters, or maybe I just feel suddenly very anxious and alone and need a hand squeeze or a kind word. Having extra supplies to share can make all the difference between a good protest experience and a really tough one.

Also, bring tissues. Hopefully you don't need them, but sometimes you end up kettled for a while and if you need to pee, you're just shit out of luck. Have tissues. You'll thank me.

IF YOU'VE BEEN ARRESTED

I am lucky enough and privileged enough to have avoided getting arrested at a protest, so I can't give my personal experience to what that is like. Instead, I'm going to tell you what I have been told by members of the National Lawyers Guild: don't tell the police anything you don't have to! In the United States, the police do not have any legal requirement to tell you the truth about why you are being arrested, and if you do anything that may be considered resisting arrest you could find yourself with additional charges. Try to write down the names and badge numbers of the officers arresting you and give them the bare minimum: your government name, ID, date of birth, address. Also, let them know about any pressing medical needs. After that? Say "I am invoking my right to remain silent. I am invoking my right to talk to a lawyer." Then remain silent. Any information you volunteer afterward can be used against you, so don't give them anything to work with! Also, don't accept drinks, gum, cigarettes, etc. from the cops while in custody—the police can and do use these for DNA samples. Finally, of course, don't talk to your cellmates about anything that led to your arrest, so you don't accidentally talk yourself into a conviction.

This advice is specific to the United States. Further detailed information varies from state to state and even place to place. I recommend learning about your local laws regarding protests, what counts as a misdemeanor and what is considered a felony, and what your rights are in your location. In the United States, the websites of the National Lawyers Guild and the ACLU are good places to learn more.

AFTER THE PROTEST

So, you've come home from the protest, taken a shower, put on clean clothes, plugged in your phone and sat down at long last. What now?

What you might need after being out in the streets varies widely. Different people respond to protests in different ways. Some folks get really fired up and find their batteries charged after an action and are eager to get out there doing bail support or other mutual aid, while others (like me) need a bit of time and quiet to re-center themselves. What are some ways to make sure your own oxygen mask is on, so you can take care of your protest buddies and wider community while decompressing?

An emotional check-in is valuable as a first step. Protests can be really dysregulating and overstimulating! You may feel dissociated and as if the protest was unreal or dreamlike. You may feel intense bursts of emotion, or you might feel numb. You may feel fierce pride and joy at how it went, or you may feel betrayed, angry or confused. You may find yourself combing through the experience for what you think you should have done differently. Taking a moment to check in with yourself can help you figure out what you might need in terms of support and care.

I personally like to use my time in the shower to do a body scan, checking whether there are any areas of my body that feel especially tight or sore. Is it easy for me to focus on the water coming down over my body, or do I find my thoughts scattered? How is my breathing? Knowing where I'm at can help me know what I may need, and how much extra energy I may have to spare for others. I may do some extra slow and gentle stretching, with a loving focus on my feet, calves and shoulders (especially if I was carrying a heavy pack). Some folks also find icing or soaking their feet helps mitigate the soreness that can come from walking for hours.

Then, I like to make sure I'm well fed. Getting some balanced nutrients in my system does wonders for my mental and physical health. I often try to eat food high in magnesium and/or potassium to help my muscles recover: spinach, sweet potatoes and bananas. If you're someone who thrives with social time, it might be good to feed your comrades, making a meal together and talking about how you think the protest went and what you'd like to adapt for next time. If you're someone who prefers alone time, cooking for yourself can be a nice, focused meditation to keep you in the moment. I also like to have a cup of herbal tea, which helps me feel grounded and soothed.

Part of my post-protest routine is listening to music, watching a show or enjoying a fun podcast, perhaps while stretching. Remember that pleasure is an important part of activism too?

This is a great time to engage that! Some folks like to journal about their experiences (though remember, don't put anything on the internet that you wouldn't want to be read in court, about you or your comrades).

Trying to get some rest is also vital, though it can be hard to do after an action. You may find yourself filled with restlessness and anxiety, even if you're physically tired. I've been known to take melatonin gummies, do a short meditation, listen to a sleep podcast or read to help my brain calm down and get ready to sleep. Using a sleep mask also helps me signal to my body that it's time to settle down, even when it feels like a toddler having a sleep-deprived tantrum.

Scheduling check-ins with your protest buddies for the next week or two is a good idea, and it's something that can easily slip your mind in the aftermath. I like to set myself some little reminders on my calendar app to send a text just to see how everyone is doing. It offers an opportunity for people to advocate for what they need, and it reminds people that we care about each other outside of the protest space.

Processing our experiences with other people is one way to ease post-protest trauma that many people find useful. This could be with a therapist, a fellow activist, a family member or a friend. I encourage you to find either someone who was there with you and can hold space from that perspective or someone who is able and willing to just listen without offering advice unless asked. If at all possible, do this voice-to-voice, instead of by text. It's even better if you can do it in person. And remember to be compassionate with yourself—you can strive to be a little better today than you were yesterday while also knowing perfection isn't an achievable goal.

It can be hard to figure out exactly what you need when you're in an emotional state—I know I've sometimes felt an intense chemical crash after the adrenaline of an action. Take a look at the resources in the back of the book to help you figure out what you may need and to also figure out what kind of help you may be able to offer others.

The last chapter of this book is specifically about burnout because whether you're going to protests, or talking to family members about difficult topics, or struggling with injustice in a professional setting, pacing yourself is absolutely key. If thinking about your activism makes you want to crawl back into bed, feel free to skip to that chapter! The rest of the book will be here for you when you're ready.

QUESTIONS

* What kind of protest roles do you feel
  you could confidently fit into?
* What are some roles that would not be a good fit?
* What is a protest skill you have that you can teach others?
* What skill would you like to learn more about?
* Do you have a group of friends and companions
  you would feel safe protesting with?
  ⊙ What roles do they fill well?
* How can you take care of yourself physically and
  emotionally after an intense experience?

CHAPTER 8:
RISKY BUSINESS: NAVIGATING DIFFERENT STRATEGIES

We've talked a bit about how to make sure you're taking care of yourself and those around you in a sustainable way. We've talked about how to navigate power disparities and social advantages, and how to recognize and value all different kinds of contribution to a cause. We've talked about exploring some of these concepts with your family (however you define that) and figuring out what forms of communication work and what don't. We've even talked about how to figure out what kind of activism is sustainable for you. That's all well and good, but what do you do when you and your loved ones believe in wildly different strategies when it comes to saving the world? How do you work together, and do you even need to?

I firmly believe in coalition building and recognizing that progress requires a variety of responses and approaches, both to keep that progress steadily moving forward and also to ensure the whole community can work together. That's certainly simpler to hold onto as an ideal when we have the same ultimate end goals.

For example, I consider myself an anarchosyndicalist, even though I still participate in voting and local politics. Some folks don't vote as part of their ideology. I do because I figure it's worth participating in the system we're currently in even while striving to move beyond it. I can usually easily work with other anarchosyndicalists. In general (and in theory), we have the same end goal of achieving a stateless society that both recognizes the value of individual choice and the power of workers to define their own guidelines and worth for their labor.

However, most anarchosyndicalists I know are long-term dreamers, academics and/or members of the working class. I certainly organize alongside them and am happy to count myself among them, but I also know that there is no ideological purity in being poor and miserable. Activists with the same ideology as me are often passing around the same $5 for who-ever needs it the most today—a heartfelt type of mutual aid. We're all hustling for resources and struggling to survive, which makes bigger scales of activism feel unachievable. So, when it comes to certain issues, I often reach out a hand beyond people I share that identity with, including people that my fellow anarchosyndicalists might initially find horrifying.

One example of this is my best friend, a libertarian with whom I have many friendly and lively debates about what the structure of society should (will?) be. She's very pro-capitalism and I'm pretty against it, so we're unlikely to be perfect allies on that topic. I imagine we'll be in rocking chairs continuing to debate on the merits of the free market! But when it comes to being against military spending, against qualified immunity for the police, in support of drug decriminalization or in support of abortion rights access, we are *attuned enough*. So, that's what we collaborate on, when appropriate. We don't have to agree on everything, not even the ultimate end goal—we just have to ride to the next bus stop together. By combining our different viewpoints and resources, we are able to form a coalition that can reach more people, and by not trying to change each other, we can stay friends and allies without feeling like we have to pretend to be someone we aren't.

There is another side benefit to this, which is that forming these coalitions and having them succeed also creates a bond of trust between us, which makes it possible for us to have healthy discussions and disagreements about long-term strategy. Rather than being stuck in echo chambers, we listen and learn from each other, sometimes expanding our perspective to include things we may not have considered before and also strengthening our positions from a more educated place. Our conversations have led me to read more about capitalism as a theory, which has helped me better articulate what concerns me about it without falling so easily into logical fallacies. My friend says that as a result of our discussions, she better understands the ways the market would need to ensure not to leave disenfranchised people behind, like folks with disabilities. Our willingness to engage and even to disagree helps us be better, more rounded activists in our own spheres, even if our methodologies differ.

I had a similar experience with a partner who felt very strongly that he wanted to be on the front lines of the Abolish ICE protests. I felt that, for me, it was a high-risk, low-reward situation, and I wasn't going to attend for that reason, though I supported him following his heart. We knew that we had different physical capabilities, different financial and social responsibilities, and different strategies for protests we considered effective. Rather than argue about the validity or value of the action, we found ways to support each other and compromise. I agreed to be his one phone call so he could get home if he were arrested, and I didn't have to be participate in something that made me uncomfortable. We didn't try to change each other's minds or shame each other, but instead met each other where we were at.

This is perhaps easier to do in cases where people are close to each other outside of their activism, and therefore have a shared love and investment in each other. But I have also found this kind of emotional step back to be helpful in better understanding people who have wildly different beliefs than I do. One example of that is anti-porn feminism. I was in the adult industry for fourteen years in various capacities, and I was a sex worker rights activist during that time as well. Clashing with anti-porn feminists online was a frustrating and futile endeavor, especially when I was younger and more invested in being heard than I was in listening. And it wasn't unreasonable for me to be angry. Frankly, I was personally experiencing the industry they condemned, and I found their complaints to be infantilizing and uninformed.

Then, on a whim, I started reading some of the texts that they held as sacred to their beliefs: *Not For Sale: Feminists Resisting Prostitution and Pornography*, edited by Christine Stark and Rebecca Whisnant, was one such book. An anthology that covers a range of voices, from people who had been in the industry to social theorists to feminist academics, this book was on the surface the polar opposite to my own experiences and beliefs about sexuality and the adult industry. Many of the premises the text took for granted—that sex work is always and inherently exploitative, that it comes from men's contempt for women, that it is "selling your body"—are not things I agree with, even with my experience of having been, at times, a survival sex worker who counted on the work to pay for food and housing.

But I didn't just dismiss the book out of hand. I kept reading. What I heard was women expressing concern that sex work was sometimes the only viable way for a low-income, undereducated single mother to take care of her kids. I found myself agreeing that a lack of support for disenfranchised women did create a situation that bad actors could easily exploit. The editors of *Not For Sale* may want to address that problem by making sex work illegal and increasing social stigma for people who purchase sex work. I want to address that problem by decriminalizing sex work so that people who do find themselves in that situation don't have to fear the police and so sex workers feel like they can report crimes against them. We disagree on what to do about that problem, but we do agree that it is a problem. Perhaps we could work together on a project that would increase childcare options and educational opportunities for people who are looking to leave the adult industry without either compromising our beliefs.

It is much easier to hold that kind of compassionate space now that I have built up my own resilience and know myself in a secure and stable way. When I was in my early twenties, being accused of being a bad feminist would have made me defensive, like I had something to prove. Now, I find myself more able to approach such an accusation with curiosity and good faith—I would want to ask why they felt that way, to assess what behaviors led them to that conclusion. I might uncover something about myself, such as an unexamined bias, that would create an opportunity for education and growth. Or, after doing my due diligence, I might realize that the accusation had more to do with the person casting it than it had to do with me. Either way, I lose nothing when I listen with a curious and open mind, and sometimes, I gain a powerful perspective that helps me do a little bit better today than I did yesterday.

While it can be incredibly powerful and effective to work towards a common goal alongside people and communities who have a different perspective, it can also be emotionally exhausting. Hell, just talking to people who have different politics or strategies can be exhausting, especially when you're trying to approach them in good faith, and they don't seem to be adopting the same attitude. Many people experienced this with QAnon, a conspiracy theory whose core belief is summarized by Wikipedia as "a cabal of Satanic, cannibalistic child molesters is operating a global child sex trafficking ring that conspired against President Donald Trump." The rise of QAnon tore families apart, and while in 2025 I don't see it explicitly discussed so much anymore, I do hear many of the beliefs QAnon popularized in online comments—the idea that aborted fetuses are being used as skin care, for example, or that billionaire philanthropist George Soros pays leftist protesters to show up for different events. When someone believes in these things, trying to work with them on something you both agree on, like feeding the poor, may still be too much contact, especially if they keep trying to convert you to their side.

Biting your tongue to keep the peace can feel infuriating when the person you're talking to shares beliefs you find abhorrent, whether it's a loved one, a coworker or a comrade. It isn't always worth it, either! I think I have a block list on my social media that's longer than my friends list. My anxiety and blood pressure spike when I'm trying to shove down my inner social justice paladin, especially if the issue being discussed matters deeply to me. While I am a fan of opening up my social sphere to people who are different from me, I'm also very firm with my boundaries when it comes to others treating me and those I care about with respect.

How, then, do you let people be different and have different opinions on how to handle the world without silencing yourself and feeling complicit, or having a panic attack whenever a potentially difficult topic comes up because you're anticipating a fight? When you figure it out, can you let me know?

Jokes aside, I do have some strategies for demonstrating that I am interested in engaging in good faith, assessing if the other person is also interested in that and disengaging when necessary. I'm also adding in some advice for harm reduction that can be applied if you love someone who does riskier types of actions than you do, because that can also be a point of friction.

First, let's talk about figuring out what your boundaries are. I remember the day I read this on the website Captain Awkward:

> My personal epiphany around setting
> boundaries involved realizing that I
> could live with a family member's deep
> and abiding disappointment, but I would
> no longer show up to participate in my
> own mistreatment. Shutting this kind of
> pressure down is less about preventing
> people from trying it, and much more
> about deciding that come what may, you're
> not rewarding it, and everyone will have
> to get used to some disappointment.

It completely blew my mind. The reframing of biting my tongue as participating in my own mistreatment so as to avoid disappointing family (or someone else I was close to) was absolutely revolutionary for me. It reminded me that *my comfort also matters*. It also reminded me that keeping the peace at my own expense was also a disappointment, because it disappointed me and my own ethics. This reframe not only applied to issues I considered personal (LGBTQ+ issues, for example, or fatphobia) but also issues that were important and impactful to my loved ones (racism or transphobia). Captain Awkward also reminds us to "never debate human rights with people who don't think you have them." It's a good rule, and helpful when trying to figure out whether something is a line in the sand for you. "Everyone has a right to their opinions" also includes you, and if someone gives other people the benefit of the doubt but not you, that may well be a red flag.

It's also useful to figure out the power dynamics at play. It's a lot easier for me to avoid contentious topics with a family member I don't speak to often and who doesn't have any influence over my life than it is to navigate those same topics with someone I live with. If I set a boundary, do I believe the other person will give me the respect of following it? Do I feel like I can be honest about how something makes me feel? If we really can't be in the same space together, can I walk away from the situation? Knowing how much agency I have helps me figure out how comfortable and safe I feel putting my foot down.

Thinking about how much agency the other person has is also useful here. For example, I am the master tenant in my apartment, so if a roommate and I have a disagreement and realize that someone has to move out, it's going to be the roommate. Therefore, I am more conscious about what topics I casually discuss with my roommate, and I make sure to ask for consent before I start going off about current events so they can opt out if they wish. I am aware that they may feel pressured to put up with my banter about politics or risk losing their home. I know I wouldn't kick them out for disagreeing with me, but they don't know that! My current housemate and I came up with an agreement to ask if the other person has ten minutes to talk about a current political issue so that we can give informed consent or bow out if it's not a good time. In this way, we can let each other be different, talk about big issues sometimes, but also not cause friction in our living situation if I want to talk about white nationalism and she just wants to cook dinner.

This also holds up when organizing together. My best friend and I disagree about the value of capitalism, but when we're strategizing about reproductive rights access, we can discuss and plan around many issues without debating capitalism, so we do that. Do I think capitalism makes a difficult situation even harder by making preventative healthcare inaccessible? Absolutely. Can we still work together on trying to maintain Plan B access? Yes. By focusing on our similarities and not arguing our differences, we can do *something* without feeling exhausted by each other in the process. With people I'm less close to but need to collaborate with, and with issues that aren't inherent to the work we're doing together, I might just redirect focus to the places we agree and leave it at that.

Another strategy I use with good results is taking the conversation private, whether online or in real life. I've found that a lot of arguments with acquaintances online spiral out of control because we're both trying to push the other to believe what we believe and are getting increasingly angry. This not only leads us to be in a position of attack/defend but doing it in public also puts us in a position of feeling like we need to double down. If I am genuinely invested in a conversation with this person, I will try to take the conversation to direct messages, where it's easier to listen and learn the "why" of their beliefs without getting as amped up. I've found that this good faith strategy often leaves people who initially violently disagreed with me saying, "Huh, I never thought of it that way. I'm going to sit with this for a while." Hell, sometimes that person is me.

When the person I disagree with is the loved one of someone close to me, or a coworker or an organizer I work alongside, that kind of patience and willingness to approach with curiosity can be a game changer. Sometimes when a person says something troubling on social media, they're just repeating something they heard, and if I gently nudge at that belief, it falls apart. And sometimes, I realize that *I* was missing a crucial piece of information and I also change my mind. That said, it's important to use this strategy with the understanding that it's not about changing each other but seeing each other.

QUESTIONS

* Have you been in a situation where you and someone close to you had different strategies for showing up as activists?
    ◉ How did you navigate that?
    ◉ What was productive about that experience and what wasn't?
* How could you work with others without compromising your beliefs or theirs?
* What are some boundaries you could develop for yourself that would help with this kind of navigation in the future?

PART FOUR:
GET ORGA-NIZED

CHAPTER 9:
WITH GREAT POWER...
(ON LEADERS)

Let's talk about leadership. But before that, let's talk about cults.

I've been doing a lot of research on cults over the last few years. I'll admit to being fascinated after reading up on recent cults of conspiracy, like QAnon and flat earthers and even Gamergate. From there, I devoured documentaries on Heaven's Gate and Jonestown (two cults that committed mass suicide) and Scientology. I initially entered my research curious but, I'll admit, a little judgmental. How could people get so lost, believe such obvious lies, be so easily manipulated? Couldn't they see that they were being used? And how was it possible that the followers of these groups didn't know their leaders were calculating and cruel?

The more I learned, the more I understood. If anything, I was taken aback by how well I understood and how easily I could see myself—had seen myself—falling into the first layers of similar dynamics. Even more startling, I could see my own experiences in how the leadership of many of these groups spiraled from "meaning well and trying to make a meaningful, communal change" to "protecting leadership at all costs." There but for the grace of God go I.

I was a very reluctant and disorganized community leader in my twenties and thirties. I would see injustices out in the world—in regard to sex worker rights, in regard to LGBTQ+ rights, in regard to consent in alternative communities—and I would decide that I wanted to do something about them. A noble goal, for sure, but one that very quickly burned me out until there was very little left. The people I was trying to help often needed sustained institutional help, like social welfare, universal healthcare or consistent income and these were not really things I, an individual who was scraping by myself, could provide. But I would try to be a one-stop shop for bleeding heart interventions anyway. I put a lot of pressure on myself to be present for every cause I cared about, showing up to protests for a range of issues from abortion rights to land-back initiatives (which aim to return land rights to Indigenous groups), cooking for unhoused people, writing articles about transgender protections and talking about cybersecurity and "real names" policies with social media companies (arguing on behalf of the many people who need to use a name that doesn't match their official ID, whether because they're trans, a sex worker, a performance artist or for other reasons). If I didn't like how the local sober group handled things, I would volunteer to take more work so I could help change that. If I was frustrated by the gaps in animal welfare at the local shelter, I would join the board of directors. Oh, there isn't a reliable crisis line for people feeling unsafe? I made myself available.

Because I would show up, and I would show up consistently, I became a load-bearing pillar of the community for far too many causes. I couldn't stand to not help if I thought I could do something, but I had a very hard time saying no to anyone in need. At the same time, I felt important—people needed me and I thought I needed that in order to have value. I began to see my friends as a means to an end, the gears in the back of my brain constantly running to try and connect this person to that resource, trying to figure out what was the most effective way to push the people around me to join me in helping others. Sometimes it worked, and sometimes it led to fights, tears and loneliness. I felt like if I ever stepped away from the work, no one would care about me at all, so I kept taking on more than I could manage. It led to a complete emotional breakdown in 2012, and putting myself back together again took years. In some ways, I think I'm still doing it.

One of the last things I did in my thirties was an experiment related to my research of cults. Was it possible to run an "ethical cult"? What would that mean? How would you run it? How would you avoid the pitfalls of egoism, mismanagement of funds, abuse of power over others and government intervention? When a man with tech wealth approached me and asked if I wanted to co-found a "cult" that would be a subversive care network for sex workers, I thought it would be a good opportunity to see if it was possible to make a cult that was good for people.

Of course, I expressed concern that every group like this might start with some good intentions but warp into many of the same issues—a charismatic leader would try to protect themselves from criticism and loneliness by having relationships with members, using money for reckless and self-serving hedonism and ostracizing anyone who complained. The co-founder said I would be the CEO, the main one in charge, that I would have a stake in the "cult," like a startup might offer shares in return for labor. I made it clear that my labor was not free, so he paid me to write an FAQ, design stickers and create a back-end strategy. I rather naively thought that since I was an anarchist, atheist and asexual, it would be pretty difficult to pull the wool over my eyes.

I gave it my best shot. I tried to ensure that people who worked for us were compensated—not someday, but today. I started to work on establishing a board of directors that was entirely comprised of community leaders of other local nonprofits, people who didn't know me socially and therefore wouldn't feel intimidated by me (I hoped). I made it easy for people to write in their concerns anonymously, had guidelines for how we would hold each other accountable from a place of tough love, encouraged contractors to keep records and researched what sort of paperwork nonprofits required.

Sometimes I worked longer than I agreed to, but I figured that sometimes when you start something new, it means long hours. Sometimes the co-founder would call me with wild monologues about spirituality and feeling driven to help others, but I figured it was just a difference in how we related to community building. The co-founder would also tell me I was remembering incorrectly what we had committed to do, or what our next goal was, but I dismissed that as perhaps an aspect of my ADHD. The lawyer and the financial advisor I had been told we were working with were suddenly replaced, but I figured that I was just an activist, and I didn't know how to run an organization like this, and maybe those decisions needed to be made.

This was 2016–2017, when sex workers were fighting multiple battles for safety and rights, especially online. FOSTA (Fight Online Sex Trafficking Act) and SESTA (Stop Enabling Sex Traffickers Act) were both marketed as bills that would help prevent sex traffickers from exploiting victims, in part by suspending Section 230 of the Communications Decency Act, thus making online platforms accountable if they were found to have trafficked people on their sites. Rather than helping survivors of trafficking, many of these platforms sidestepped the law by just banning sex workers (and, in some cases, sex educators and queer people as well). Popular advertising spaces like Craigslist and Backpage removed their adult personals, which made advertising online impossible for many of the most marginalized in the adult industries. I didn't necessarily trust my co-founder's judgment, but I was excited to have financial resources available to build something sustainable for local sex workers who were reeling after bills like FOSTA/SESTA were passed.

Then the pandemic hit, and at-risk people in the community needed food delivery. I suggested to my co-founder that we could channel some money into helping a group that was running a food distribution hub and could really use the funds. My co-founder was very reluctant to do this, claiming that he had his own ideas for distribution and fundraising, that he had found a space to rent and that he could do this himself instead. I got really frustrated because I couldn't understand why he would demand that we reinvent the wheel during a time when people needed mutual aid more than ever. Why not support an existing group instead? "Because no one would know we were the ones doing it!" he cried during one fateful phone call, and I felt a lightning strike of realization.

And that's how they get you, folks. I realized that I had been ignoring the writing on the wall, which was revealing a co-founder who was emotionally insecure, who believed God was talking to him, who was not respecting my clearly outlined boundaries. He didn't want to help people because he wanted to help people. He wanted to be seen as a savior of the disenfranchised. "Oh shit," I said to myself, "this 'cult' is now just a *cult,* no scare quotes required." Just in case, and to confirm my concerns, I talked to everyone I knew was working with us. I figured out who was supposedly our current legal and financial counsel and talked to them (they were not being paid, just friendly with the co-founder and wanted to help a charitable cause). I talked to sex workers who were supposedly consulting on various aspects of how to help the wider population, only to find that the co-founder was paying them for sex work more often than for consultations. People weren't coming to me with their concerns because they thought I was a hundred percent behind the co-founder. I realized that I was not a co-founder, and maybe had never had power in this organization, but was instead a beard for a tech guy with money to hide behind. I was a figurehead of consent culture and activism, which meant that marginalized people trusted him because he was working with me. Realizing this was like a stab in the heart.

I quit and wrote an email to everyone I knew of who worked with the group to explain why I was resigning and what I thought the dangers were. I outlined what boundaries had been crossed and apologized for how I enabled all of it. "I came onto this project to see if it was possible to create an ethical cult," I said. "And now I know the answer: No."

I got out before it got really bad, before I could be held legally responsible for the behavior of my co-founder, before I could be audited and before I ended up arrested. I got everyone I could out too. Many joined because I was there, and they believed in me (something that initially felt like an honor, and something that I later looked back on in horror). I wrote publicly about my accountability around the founding and running of the group and my concerns about the abuses of power by the co-founder. I invited people to contact me if they needed to. Years later, I still get stories from people who had bad experiences with this guy. I wish my desire to do a thought experiment hadn't hurt people, and I will continue to offer restitution and assistance to anyone impacted by the ripple effect of my naivete.

Why am I writing about this? After all, this is a book about activism and relationships, not cults or high-control groups. Well, that experience taught me a lot about the responsibility that comes from being in leadership—and no matter how much you might say a group has horizontal leadership, where everyone leads each other, humans tend to organize themselves into hierarchies. When you don't talk about who is in charge of what, how everyone else can hold them accountable to their agreements and what will happen if they don't accept accountability, you run a genuine risk of having an unspoken structure where those with the most power—money, whiteness, experience, etc.—are in charge, with no checks and balances in place to even the scales or address harm.

As Jo Freeman writes in *The Tyranny of Structurelessness*:

> This means that to strive for a
> structureless group is as useful,
> and as deceptive, as to aim at an
> "objective" news story, "value-free"
> social science, or a "free" economy.
> A "laissez-faire" group is about as
> realistic as a "laissez-faire" society;
> the idea becomes a smokescreen for
> the strong or the lucky to establish
> unquestioned hegemony over others. This
> hegemony can be so easily established
> because the idea of "structurelessness"
> does not prevent the formation of
> informal structures, only formal ones.
> Similarly "laissez-faire" philosophy did
> not prevent the economically powerful

from establishing control over wages,
prices, and distribution of goods; it
only prevented the government from doing
so. Thus structurelessness becomes a
way of masking power, and within the
women's movement is usually most strongly
advocated by those who are the most
powerful (whether they are conscious
of their power or not). As long as the
structure of the group is informal, the
rules of how decisions are made are known
only to a few and awareness of power
is limited to those who know the rules.
Those who do not know the rules and are
not chosen for initiation must remain
in confusion, or suffer from paranoid
delusions that something is happening
of which they are not quite aware.

After that experience, "leadership" is a role I try to avoid as much as possible, and if I do take it on, I make sure the rules are very explicit and clear to all—not just how to opt-in, but how to opt-out. I wish I could say it's simply because I don't want power, but if I'm really honest, it's not that. I certainly have my egotistical moments of thinking that if only everyone did what I told them, they'd have a much easier time of it! I usually don't want to be a leader because there's a lot of responsibility in being the main person people look to for answers, and I get exhausted by it faster than anything else. I regularly tried to find ways to share power, accountability and responsibility with a group of people, both out of a desire to embrace a diversity of opinions and to ensure that the group could move forward without everyone being present, but it was just as much about trying to avoid the resentment that can come from regularly being "the reliable one." I have learned that a major part of leadership is listening more than you talk, asking people how they want to show up and honoring that and then stepping back and training people so they can step forward.

Critical thinking is a fundamental part of being a human in the world, and it's just as important when it comes to thinking about leadership, both what kind of leader you want to be and what kind of leader is safe to follow. One of the best tools I read about during my cult research was the BITE model, developed by Dr. Steven Hassan (a licensed mental health professional and recognized expert on cults) to assess whether a group was potentially high control. He considers:

Behavior: How the group manipulates and regulates people's behavior through strict and unquestionable rules, individual and community-wide punishments, and unpredictable rewards.

Information: How the group controls information coming in or going out, limiting members' access to outside perspectives and steeping them in propaganda.

Thought: How the group uses psychological tactics to shut down critical thinking and encourage conformity, often shaping the beliefs and behaviors of the group to only trust fellow members.

Emotion: How the group fosters emotional attachment and codependency through love bombing, guilt and fear, such as by requiring confessions of "failings" and labeling some feelings as "bad."

When I considered this model and my relationship to the group I was in, I could easily see the beginning of "Emotion" manipulation beginning to take root. The co-founder used guilt to push my buttons and had a total lack of accountability. I figured I had nipped it in the bud, that I had observed it accurately. But on researching more deeply, I began to see there were a few other red flags: the financial dependency he cultivated by giving me this work as my day job, which I needed to pay rent, was part of "Behavior," and his gaslighting me about my memories of our conversations and agreements was a red flag for "Thought." While he wasn't very effective at creating a high-control group—in part because he was very disorganized and somewhat manic—I could see how these things start if you don't know what to look for. Given a little more time, it may have been a much more dangerous situation.

Now, let's bring all of this out of the world of cults and into the world of interpersonal relationships and group dynamics. You see, keeping an eye out for these kinds of control tactics is not only useful for cults, but also for being mindful of the ways others are trying to influence us and how we are trying to influence others. Being aware of these manipulative behaviors is an important step to addressing them, whether they're being used against one person in a couple, a small organizing unit or a spiritual community. "You'll never find people who accept you like I/we do" is a powerful control tactic, whatever the context. "You're only valuable as long as you do as I/we say" is toxic as hell.

Remember that whole thing about how "the only person we can control is ourselves"? Part of why I wanted to address this dynamic in this book is because I've seen the isolating ripple effect go through communities, over and over again. While bad actors do exist, I think we are also often indirectly influenced to behave in these controlling ways by watching those around us, the media we consume, even our fellow activists on social media. "If you don't change this behavior, then we're going to cancel and thus shun you" *can* be an effective last resort, an ultimate consequence for someone who isn't responding to feedback any other way, but all too often I see it used as a bludgeon by people who care more about, as activist Ashtin Berry says, "being right versus being in right relationship." This dynamic can cultivate that moral scrupulosity that leaves people feeling powerless and hopeless, instead of compassionately inspiring them to do better by your actions.

So, now that we know how *not* to act in leadership, let's examine what responsible leadership looks like. I would not consider myself an expert on this by any means, but there are a few things I look for when deciding how active I want to be in an organizing group.

Forbearing: How do the leaders respond to the group when leadership takes a wrong step? Are they patient and eager to educate, or do they scold and shut people down? Do they encourage personal growth or unquestioning obedience? Do the leaders have each other's (and the rest of the group's) backs, even when they fuck up, and especially when they disagree with each other?

Accountable: How do the leaders hold themselves accountable when they screw up? Do they have a third party to step in, so they aren't able to just handwave away the issues of their co-leaders? How do the leaders give and receive feedback? If the leaders have been held accountable in the past, did the group feel good about how that went?

Transparent: How do the leaders set out guidelines for the group? Is it a shared process or top-down? Who manages the finances, and do they share the details with the group? How do decisions get made? How did the leaders become the leaders? What behavior would cause a leader of this group to be ousted? How do new leaders get voted in?

Humble: How do the leaders respond to feedback in the moment? Are they accessible to the rest of the group to speak directly, or do they hold themselves apart? Are they actively involved in actions in some capacity, or do they give everyone else stuff to do? Do they educate themselves on how to act in allyship with the disenfranchised? Do they listen more than talk?

Adaptive: How do the leaders respond when someone says they can't do something or don't want to? Is it their way or the highway, or do they find another method? Do they use shame to try and push back against people's stated boundaries? If something goes sideways at an action, can they adapt to the needs of the moment or do they stubbornly dig their heels in?

Generous: How do the leaders give back to the community? Do they make sure to train up others into areas of responsibility? Do they want to be the only leader or one of many leaders and thus foster leadership in others? Are they quick to offer constructive feedback, compliments and assistance?

These considerations are really just a starting place, but I find groups that raise up leaders who care about these things and prioritize them are far more likely to be healthy groups to work with. Feeling an investment in yourself, in those around you and in the community in which you organize is such an important aspect of leadership to me. And I cannot tell you how many groups I've been a part of that fell apart because leaders didn't want to be transparent about how they spent money or elected themselves to positions of power and refused to train others or share responsibility, or they saw themselves as above the group they were leading and above accountability. I think a good leader adopts the campsite rule, but with others instead of parks—they leave people better than they found them. Preferably, the group is left with the skills and confidence to lead their own effective actions based on their own passions.

Many of the things I value in a leader and try to foster in my own leadership are not only for the good of the community, but for the care and feeding of the leaders themselves. An activism pod that is invested in shared responsibility and mutual care is going to be more capable to lead themselves when a leader needs or wants to step away. Knowing that a group I'm leading trusts me to listen to feedback and be flexible in the moment helps me trust them to have my back at an action even when it gets hairy. I'm a lot less likely to burn out if I feel like I can take some time away to recharge without the work slowing to a stop. I have never felt more anxious and trapped than when I realized that some vital form of community aid would disappear if I didn't keep it alive. At the same time, I've certainly had partners and friends who felt frustrated that they didn't get to spend social time with me because I was so exhausted and cranky from being "on" all the time. We have to care for ourselves in order to best care for others, and we have to let others care for us, too.

QUESTIONS

* Can you think of a time when you encountered a leader or other authority figure who creeped you out?

- What sort of behaviors did you hear about or witness that led to you feeling that way?
- Does the BITE model give you a new perspective on this person or experience?

* What are some leadership qualities you have grown to really value?
  - Do you see any of those leadership qualities in yourself?

CHAPTER 10:
...COMES GREAT RESPONSIBILITY (ON STEPPING UP)

Now that I've talked some about what to consider when looking at the ethics of a leader as an individual, let's also talk about the role the leader holds as a facilitator and steward for the community they lead. Consider not only what kind of leader you want, but what kind of leadership relationship you want. The answers will inform a lot of how you organize and plan projects. They can also help you get more in touch with what kind of leader you are drawn to being yourself, if you so choose. I am a firm believer that almost everyone has the capacity to be an excellent leader in certain contexts or for a certain amount of time, if they want to step into the role.

When I first begin to figure out the structure of group collaboration, whether it's a potluck dinner or a multistage accountability process, I start with a discussion of how we want to handle leadership. I've learned that an ounce of prevention (and conversation) is worth a pound of cure. Or, more accurately, by discussing and laying out how we want the structure of the community to come together to work in practice, what that means to us and how we'll take on our individual roles, we can prevent a lot of disappointment and frustration down the line. There are lots of different ways to organize, including how we talk to each other about ideas, how we decide on a path forward and how we hold each other accountable for our responsibilities. Here, I'm going to offer some basic strategies and tools that might resonate with you. Feel free to adapt them to your specific needs. What may be perfect for running a first aid resource for unhoused folks may be really ineffective for applying pressure to a local politician!

Different types of leadership styles have benefits and drawbacks when people apply them to community organizing. To prevent conflict, it's worth making sure that the people you're working with have the same vision as you for how leadership will work. I recommend considering which of these models sounds most effective for you and your goals. If you do find yourself in a position of leadership, it's important to not only reflect on what kind of relationship you as a leader may want with your community, but also what kind of leadership your community is seeking from you.

Democratic: In an ideal democratic leadership structure, decision-making is shared by the community. Open communication, cooperation and involvement is encouraged, with either a community-selected leader who enacts the will of the community, a revolving leadership voted for on a schedule, or no leader at all.

Advantages: Everyone has a vote, which increases the feeling of investment. The community feels heard and directly involved in which projects go forward and how they're structured. Active participation can feel inspiring, and a diverse array of ideas are often put forward for consideration.

Disadvantages: Everyone has a vote, meaning decision-making can take much longer. Active participation can be draining when no resolution is passed. If there is a lack of unanimity, a project can wither on the vine while the community debates. Anarchists joke a lot about this strategy as being "having meetings about meetings."

Autocratic: In an ideal autocratic leadership structure, an individual makes all the decisions and delegates the necessary tasks. The leader makes decisions based on their own judgment and rarely solicits feedback from the community. This strategy is about as effective as the trust the community has for an autocratic leader.

Advantages: Decisions are made swiftly, which can be a major plus during a crisis as there isn't a need to wait for consensus. The leader can clearly lay out expectations and participants can easily lay accountability at the feet of the autocrat in charge.

Disadvantages: Community members may feel undervalued and that their concerns are unheard. If trust is damaged, the project will likely fall apart. It's also often an appealing strategy for power-hungry people who don't make terribly effective leaders in the long term. This style is also very stressful for the leader, who bears the weight of all the decision-making and its consequences.

Transformational: In an ideal transformational leadership structure, leaders lead by example, inspiring the community through a shared purpose but with flexibility in how to get there. The leader often focuses their energy on positive reinforcement of the community and fosters curiosity, innovation and reaching individual potential.

Advantages: This is a very engaging style of leadership that encourages passion, ambitious goal-setting and creative solutions. It's a style that's all about brainstorming and blue-sky thinking, which can make people feel inspired and motivated.

Disadvantages: This is definitely an issue of seeing the big picture but not being great at details, which means that logistics can be a sticking point. Shooting for the stars may also lead to a lot of disappointment. While striving to bring out the best in yourself can be a good thing, it can also lead to burnout for the leader and the community at large, because it can feel like there's always more to do.

Laissez-Faire: In an ideal laissez-faire leadership structure, the leader may assign tasks but rely on the community to be self-motivated in how they accomplish those tasks. Members can make decisions independently, and they get the credit for success or the responsibility if those results fall short.

Advantages: When working with a group of highly motivated and skillful community members, this can be a very satisfying way to work. It encourages individual innovation and creativity in problem-solving. It makes people feel trusted to do their part of the whole and leaves them to make that happen in a way that's effective for each individual. It also can be a way to encourage people to be leaders of their own teams, building useful skills and independence.

Disadvantages: Some leaders attracted to this strategy may be a little too hands-off, leaving community members who feel out of their depth at loose ends. This can be an avoidant type of leadership where the supposed "leader" isn't really taking responsibility as a leader, which makes accountability chaotic. It can be hard to understand what everyone's role is and who to contact about what. If community members act in their own self-interest, there can be a lot of hard-to-resolve conflict.

Servant: In an ideal servant leadership structure, leaders are more like facilitators who often prioritize the needs of the community above all else. A leader using this style is focused on the development of others, listening and displaying empathy rather than telling people what to do.

Advantages: This style encourages communication, which can lead to loyalty, satisfaction and a feeling of value. Leaders feel like they are in a place of service instead of authority, which can increase the sense of community and mutual care.

Disadvantages: This style doesn't scale very well and can be disorganized in a crisis, as roles can feel fuzzy and poorly defined. It may take a long time to arrive at decisions, and if an unpopular decision needs to be made for long-term community success, it may instead fizzle if the leader lacks assertiveness. This may also leave the leader feeling like the community is taking advantage of them and pushing them to be accommodating above and beyond their capability.

Collaborative: In an ideal collaborative leadership structure, there is a leadership team who is empowered to make their own decisions for the people they lead, and who come together to craft a larger strategy.

Advantages: By breaking a big project into smaller bite-sized pieces, each leader can focus on the area they have expertise in. This strategy also allows the individual leaders to have a more personal relationship with the people they lead while still speaking to those people on behalf of the leadership team. This is also an adaptive strategy that can keep a project moving forward even if one leader drops off, because other gears are still moving.

Disadvantages: When you have many leaders, the decision-making process takes longer. Also, the smaller groups may present conflicting needs, which can create conflict amongst the leadership team. Louder voices can drown out the rest, too, which can be frustrating.

Something I have certainly found exhausting in my own community organizing is when there's an inconsistency between what the community *says* they want from leadership versus what they *respond* to. I've certainly been relieved that a group said they wanted a laissez-faire approach, but then the work just didn't get done if someone didn't nudge people. Sometimes this is an issue of people not fulfilling their commitments and sometimes it's an issue of people unintentionally overcommitting (a common struggle for those of us who care about community care). I've also left organizations when they claimed to use democratic leadership, but in practice were autocratic with very little transparency on how decisions were made, which made me feel like the time I spent at "leadership meetings" was a waste.

I feel like no one of these strategies works a hundred percent of the time, and instead, you may find yourself straddling a couple, or trying more than one before settling mostly into a particular style. I think that's pretty normal, and it's good to be patient and humble through that process while you work out the kinks. There are also ways to mitigate the negatives of these styles while playing up the positives. For example, I tend to initially organize parties in a pretty autocratic way, to ensure set up, clean up, food, drink and entertainment are all sorted in a way I am happy to manage. After I assign roles and set expectations, I also let go of my need to control every individual aspect (I don't need to outline specifically what drinks are brought to a picnic, as long as there are nonalcoholic options). This means the party will mostly go according to the plan I set out, while also allowing people to bring their own flair and relieving me of the stress of micromanagement.

It's also really important to consider how genuinely open to feedback and change of strategy you are, as a leader and as a community. What channels do you have in place to allow members of the community (or people outside of the community) to give feedback on the work you're doing? Do they have to put their name to their feedback, or is there an anonymous method? How do you handle complaints made by anonymous people, who may or may not have productive intentions? How public do you want accountability processes to be, and what level of complaint is an immediate stop and assess?

I'll be real here—while I like to say that I am open to feedback, and I do try to authentically reflect on any feedback I receive, when transmisogynists have told me that vocally including trans women in my feminist activism is a betrayal to women, I roll my eyes and get on with it anyway. Whatever work you're doing, some people will engage with you and your activism in bad faith, and you will have to make decisions about when to listen and learn and when to toss it in the garbage. But it's a good idea to think ahead of time about how your leaders (and the leadership strategy they, or you, use) will respond to criticism, both in good faith and in bad faith. If you plan ahead for it, it's a lot less likely to derail the activism you're doing, and you're less likely to burn out trying to resolve it.

Finally, the leadership strategy you put in place will inform the community of how easy it is for them to step into a position of leadership if they wish, and how acceptable it is for them to step down if it's overwhelming them. Communicating that and following through on it can help attract people to the projects you're doing. If I have a lot of stuff already on my plate, I may find myself attracted to a more autocratic leader. Then, I can just serve a need that is laid out for me without needing to think about it very much (like answering a call to weed a community garden for a day). If I have useful expertise on a project, I may look for a leadership style that will listen to and reward my ideas (like advising on social media strategy for a nonprofit).

QUESTIONS

* Have you ever been in a position of guidance or authority in the past?
    ⊙ If yes, what worked for you in that situation, and what didn't?
    ⊙ If not, in what situation could you see yourself stepping up into a leadership position?
        * What would make that feel achievable for you?
* Do any of these leadership styles sound especially attractive to you as a community member?
    ⊙ Could you see yourself using any of them, or a combination, in your own leadership of a project or a group?

CHAPTER 11:
ORGANIZE, ORGANIZE, ORGANIZE

Often, how a project functions ends up left in the hands of the "leadership" simply because the people who end up as leaders are the ones who show up the most consistently. However, I believe every community should tackle the logistical backend of how they organize, as organizers and participants together. While it's impossible to anticipate every possible conflict ahead of time, some things are pretty likely to come up: How money gets spent and tracked, what to do when someone in the group harms another, how to hold leaders accountable for their words and deeds, how the group makes decisions and follows through on them. If you put together a robust yet flexible plan that covers the main bases, it frees you up to adapt to problems when they come up and to act with transparency and consistency. That can prevent your community from arguing about the nature and repercussions of a conflict, so everyone can focus their attention on coming up with lasting solutions.

I like to put in place a few specific things when I'm organizing a group, whether for a one-time action or a longer-term project.

AN OBJECTIVE

First and foremost, it's helpful to say out loud "What's the goal of this group? Why are we coming together, and what are we hoping to accomplish?" Think about what problem you're trying to solve or alleviate, what you want to see happen instead and how you plan to get there and of course, what your vision for the future is. This can help inspire your community into action while also giving you a useful ruler by which to measure your strategy.

It can be helpful to have an overarching mission statement that communicates the goal, acting as an umbrella under which any actions and organizing fall. I think ultimately, though, it's about objectives. I like to think about objectives using a method called SMART: Specific, Measurable, Achievable, Relevant, and Time-Specific. Yeah, this comes from the world of corporate business, and yeah, I think capitalism is a hellfire from which we need to escape, but I also appreciate the stripped-down practicality of this method.

Specific: Keep your mission simple and well-defined. Every word matters, so steer clear of misinterpretations by avoiding vague language. Think about what you want to achieve, why you care, how it impacts society at large and how clear the results of your work will be.

Measurable: How can you tell that what you're doing is working? Being able to have some consistent data points that show the ways your activism is improving conditions is not only helpful for fundraising, but it will also tell your fellow activists that their work is not in vain. It's also helpful to think about whether the data can be measured by a third party, which increases accountability. For example, a harm reduction program that can provide numbers for how many sharps containers went out to the community and how many came back to be disposed of safely is providing numbers that can be confirmed by a third party with no personal stake in the results. That can be useful. It's not always possible—some types of activism are about raising awareness in an amorphous way—but it's worth thinking about.

Achievable: No matter how much planning you do and how passionate you are, if you set the objective to something that is impossible to achieve or requires resources you don't have, it will be terrible for morale and people will burn out. Can you make your mission something that other people have done before in a similar timeframe?

Relevant: Is the mission relevant to the community you want to serve? Do they also consider it important? Word your mission in a way that emphasizes working with the community rather than treating them like a group in need of rescue, or like your group knows what's best for them. Even better, find a way to make working alongside leaders of the communities you want to serve part of the mission (including creating your mission with those leaders present and involved).

Time-Specific: Is there an end to this after which we regroup and strategize again? Having a deadline helps encourage a sense of some urgency, but you want to strike a balance between it being too long (leading the group to lose momentum and fall apart) or too short (making it impossible to achieve sustainably). It also helps you assess if the objective and strategy were productive or not.

Your mission statement or objective doesn't have to stay the same forever, but this is also a good time to think about how and when you may fine-tune it. Doing so will help reduce conflict down the line while increasing a sense of transparency and investment for the people doing the work today. There's nothing as disheartening as organizing under a mission statement that feels out of touch and not having any way to update it!

A CODE OF CONDUCT

A code of conduct is a way to formalize how your community works and plays together. If the mission statement and the objective are the ideals of your group, the code of conduct covers the way this mission manifests in the practical day-to-day. What does it look like in reality? This is where you can create some guardrails for what might be called "company culture" in other contexts. A code of conduct should clearly discuss desirable and undesirable behaviors, using language that fits the general vibe of the group. It should also let people know what are "yellow card" and "red card" behaviors. What actions would lead to a warning and what actions would lead to consequences including being removed from the group?

I like any code of conduct I help create to have an addendum around how often the code of conduct is reviewed, and what the process is for adding or subtracting bits of it as a community. This encourages people to feel that everyone has their part in creating and maintaining this living document of agreements. It also keeps it adaptable and relevant to the group here now, rather than being set in stone even when the group has changed.

A FINANCIAL AGREEMENT

Money is the number one thing that I have seen pull community activist groups apart. Many activist groups require some kind of fundraising, whether it be for supplies, to rent space, to pay speakers, to bail people out or whatever the case may be. Who holds onto the money? How does the group keep track of money? Are there any checks and balances in place to make sure the group follows that tracking process? How does the group decide how to spend money? Do you tell the public how much money you have as a group, and how often do you update that number if so? When you fundraise, how are you accountable for communicating to the wider community what you spent the money on and how useful that was? Is there a way to ensure one person doesn't just run off with the money?

Creating a financial agreement is not just a good policy to increase transparency and cut down on arguments. You do *not* want to experience an IRS audit as an individual or as a group without full records of your financial activities. In the past, I've left groups that I believed in because they didn't have financial transparency. It's a huge liability.

A LEADERSHIP PLAN

I talked about this in the previous chapter about leadership, but let's say it again. How do people become leaders? How long do they stay leaders? Do you vote leaders in? Do they volunteer? What would cause the group to strip a leader of their role? What does "stripping them of their role" mean in practical terms? What is the role of the leader(s) in relation to the group as a whole? How do leaders take a break from their responsibilities to regroup? What sort of liability do leaders take on? What leadership style are you using and how flexible is it?

Figure this out when you're first creating the group and you will save yourself a lot of headaches down the line. It's not a conversation you want to have when things have gone to shit.

AN ACCOUNTABILITY PLAN

Another area of discord that I've seen time and time again is around what "accountability" means. It's probably why I write and talk about it so much! I have a lot of feelings about the word "accountability" being used to justify punishment, bullying, bad-faith arguments, etc. What does accountability mean *here*, in your group? What does it look like? What are the steps in the process?

By talking about an accountability plan in advance of anything happening, you are giving yourself and the group the opportunity to reflect on what your group's ethics are without the pressure of needing to "fix" something. It also means that when something does go wrong, you have a process to lean back on, something you've all agreed to. Taking the immediacy out of the equation helps you reflect on how you want to organize, rather than reacting. Making that plan transparent to your activist group, and even to the community at large, can allow some breathing room when conflict happens while also communicating that you are taking the issue seriously even if you don't act immediately.

You should consider how to hold people and even your activist group as a whole accountable, but you should also discuss how you reintegrate after that happens. I feel like reintegration is a piece of the puzzle often left on the floor, which is part of why everyone is so scared of it. If a leader oversteps in a way that leads the community to ask them to take a step back from leadership, think about if there is a way for them to build that trust back, and under what circumstances. If a community member makes the wrong call, ninety percent of the time, I want to give them the chance to make the right one next time. I want to let people learn, I want people to feel like they can own up when they've fucked up without feeling condemned and I want the activist community to feel invested in the outcome, so I like to structure accountability plans accordingly.

I think about this in relation to the evangelical belief about Heaven and Hell: you can spend your whole life striving to do "good" in the eyes of the Lord, but it just takes one bad thought to plunge you back down to Hell. That's not going to encourage people to be accountable for their behavior. Rather, it's going to keep them in a state of anxiety and defensiveness that stands in opposition to healthy introspection and emotional growth. It also all too often encourages everyone around them to be informants; they keep an eye on each other not to help lift each other up from a place of compassion, but rather to smugly police each other as a way to feel self-righteous. That will burn your community out about as quickly as someone running off with the money!

Put it on my gravestone: reward the behavior you want to see. More to the point, model the behavior you want to see.

A COMMUNICATION STRATEGY

The way we talk to each other can make or break an effective activist project. Think ahead of time about how people can register a complaint (and how accessible that method is). "Be compassionate with each other" sounds good, but again, what does that actually look like in practice? I've certainly seen people feel frustrated when one person believes they're offering tough but fair critique and another person feels like they're being cornered. We have to reflect not only on how to communicate with compassion, but how to receive communication with compassion (what I often call "aggressive good faith"). Insisting people talk in person may lead to someone feeling gaslighted if they don't feel the conversation is later relayed accurately, while insisting people talk via email or text may feel intimidating when screencaps can be used as weapons. Plan ahead as best you can.

Finally, I think it's helpful to consider how the group talks about their work together. Perhaps you like to establish a full, formal, *Robert's Rules* style strategy for planning (I've included some educational resources on this in the back of the book). Maybe you prefer to have an agenda and allow people to submit topics to the agenda ahead of time. Or you like to have a town hall where people gather and talk about things in a more free-form way. You might have monthly meetings or quarterly ones. You might meet for an hour or until the topics are resolved. Whatever strategy you use, communicate it upfront, be open to adapting it if someone has an accessibility issue and be consistent! These various considerations are by no means exhaustive, but they should serve to give you a solid jumping-off place for activist organizing.

Often, we are engaging in activism with our friends, our lovers and our neighbors. Spelling out strategies can help in complex situations where the lines between "fellow activist" and "person I'm close with" get blurry. Heck, you may even find some of these things helpful for planning ahead when you're visiting with difficult family for a meal, like creating a simple code of conduct that helps establish boundaries. I prefer to communicate with my housemate about house issues via email, which enables her to read about them when it's convenient and allows me to phrase things in the kindest, clearest way I can. By talking about things before they become an argument, we can give ourselves the best possible shot at avoiding conflict and a plan for how to handle it when conflict occurs.

QUESTIONS

* What are some community guidelines you have found helpful in the past?
  * What are some you found coun-terproductive, and why?
* How would you rewrite those guidelines now?
* Think of a community you are in currently and write down some core values for that community.
  * Now, come up with five guidelines for that com-munity. You might cover conflict and mediation, privacy expectations or how leaders are elected or removed.
    * How do these guidelines reflect the core values of the community?

CHAPTER 12:
TRASH FİRE: WHEN THINGS GO WRONG

No matter how much effort we put into organizing and leadership strategies and listening to each other, conflict will still flare up. I personally don't think that's a bad thing. Some amount of fire can be cleansing. Some Indigenous cultures, like the Salish in the Northern Rockies, use controlled fires to nurture the land for more productive foraging, as well as help reduce the risks of larger, less controlled fires down the line. Similarly, I think many communities benefit from "controlled burns" on occasion, to clear the dead brush and make space for fresh growth. For example, outdated thinking or traditional leadership styles might need a nudge to make way for new ideas and perspectives. There are ways to engage in that process that are about cultivation and sustainability, rather than just burning everything to the ground for the sake of it. I think we're often taught to believe that conflict is scary and destructive, but it can be something really productive and useful, especially when it can be addressed before it's been smoldering under the surface for years. As with much of my advice, you may find yourself inspired by some things I offer and dismiss others. Take what works for you and leave the rest!

I identify as a leftist: an anarchist, an antifascist, a feminist. As such, I have heard plenty of exhausted half-jokes about the left eating itself, often in response to conflict arising and people feeling scared that it will lead to the explosion of the group as a whole. I share the concern that infighting will derail a community's organization, but I don't share the fear of the conflict itself. On the contrary, I try to see conflict as an opportunity to learn, to grow in ways that may feel painful but are also often necessary, to challenge my preconceived ideas and my desire for comfort. I remind myself that criticism can often be a sign of trust—the person or people bringing the issues up believe that they will be heard and have some hope that the listeners will take action. By centering that hope instead of my feelings of defensiveness or anxiety, I can better listen to what a person is saying and figure out what I, or others, can do about it, rather than trying to shut down the conversation because I feel uncomfortable. That's not to say that bad faith criticism doesn't exist—I've had plenty of experiences with TERFs, white supremacists and racists to demonstrate that!— but I have also found that people who are criticizing in bad faith often want reactionary attention for doing so, and by not immediately being defensive, I can usually starve them of the oxygen they crave.

Bad apples do exist, and left unattended, they will poison the whole barrel. Planning for conflict resolution before you're in the thick of it and having a transparent process for accountability that the group reliably sticks to are both really helpful preemptive strategies for dealing with them. I've also found that a group can mitigate the effects of a bad actor by maintaining a living document that outlines a code of conduct for the group, regularly soliciting feedback to encourage evolution, and also creating standards and ethics that can guide the conflict resolution process. Also, it's really important to think about and address problem behaviors instead of seeing the person themselves as the problem. After all, any of us may find ourselves engaging in counterproductive behaviors, and it's a good idea to stay humble!

Recognize that legitimate dissent is healthy; try not to fall into the trap of deciding that all conflict is in bad faith or that someone is a bad apple just because you may feel defensive. You may be surprised—some of my closest friends are people who brought my attention to major issues with projects I was shepherding, and their harsh but fair feedback made my activism stronger. I value these relationships with people I can trust to call me on my shit. Seeing criticism as an opportunity for us to work together on a solution rather than a fight has helped me stay grounded in these situations and quieted my anxiety. The more you do this, the less unmoored you feel when conflict arises, which makes for a more productive discussion. It's like exercise: the more you do it, the easier it gets and the further you can go.

Have you ever seen a cross-stitched sign in a home saying "Bless this mess"? That's how I feel about conflict. It's messy, but it's also a rich and fertile ground for growth.

Now, let's break the messy business of community conflict down into two sections: reactive solutions, for after the shit has hit the fan, and proactive solutions that help to prevent shit from being near the fan to begin with.

First and foremost, how can people report an issue to the community and to the leaders? Do you have an anonymous feedback form that people can fill out online? Can they call a specific chosen person who is responsible for advocating on behalf of the person with the issue? If the issue is with a leader, is there a way to report it that isn't to the leader themself? Who holds them accountable? What is a reasonable timeline for discussion and action to be taken? What sort of follow-up can the person making the complaint expect?

I've seen a lot of people feel frustrated when someone takes the step of raising grievances publicly as a way to push some kind of response. For the person or community being called out in this way, it can sometimes feel out of the blue, especially if the person calling them out hasn't made any attempt to raise the concern privately first (sometimes called "calling in").

That said, when I've been asked to mediate situations like this, it often turns out the concerned person feels that they have previously attempted to address the issue privately and it has gone unheard, or that they don't feel safe talking about the issue privately. That lack of safety may be because the person or people they need to talk about haven't reacted well to accountability attempts in the past. It can also be an issue of transparency, where a public callout puts the issue out for all to see and weigh in on. Sometimes it feels necessary to have community support to underline that a problem is not just an individual problem, but a systemic one. It can be easier for a person or an organization to ignore or dismiss one person than to dismiss a big group.

Groups are often less likely to go straight to a public callout if they have other options for addressing conflict internally first. Are leaders available and responsive? If they need time to weigh how to respond to criticism, do they offer a concrete timeline? Are they open to various types of discussion, like an email, a text chat, a video conference or an in-person meeting? Are the leaders accommodating, which makes it easier to report? Do they allow the person raising a red flag to bring a companion for support, or allow them to record the meeting for reference? Are the policies and expectations for registering a complaint public knowledge? The more of these things you can say yes to, the more likely people are going to feel OK about discussing the issue privately and the more likely the conversation can start from a place of good faith.

It's useful to consider if criticism is coming from inside the organization, from comrades with investment in the resolution of the issue, or from outside the group. You can't necessarily wave away outsider feedback, however—there are many reasons why someone would offer criticism of a group they don't participate in. For example, they might be a former member who left because of conflict, or they could be politically opposed to the stances of the group. However, I have seen activist collectives and nonprofits fall apart when an outside person lobs an accusation just to derail the work with no desire to see a problem fixed. It doesn't happen often, and I would personally recommend taking criticism in good faith unless proven otherwise (we can always learn and grow, after all), but by recognizing that disruption can sometimes be the point, a group can more easily recenter themselves and focus on solutions rather than pessimism.

OK, so we've figured out some possible ways for people to offer feedback to individuals and the group. Is the feedback detailed and specific? I strongly recommend trying to get as much documentation as possible: when the issue occurred, if it's a pattern, how people raised the issue before and if the group did anything about it. This helps prevent you from reinventing the wheel and helps the person with the issue feel like you aren't revisiting tactics that have already failed to lead to a solution. Approach this from a place of curiosity, not accusation or defensiveness. Remember, you *want* to know the answers! This is also a good time to make sure that what you're hearing and what the other person is saying are the same through active listening, confirming notes after the meeting and getting definitions for the behaviors being discussed. "This leader has been disrespecting Black members" could mean a variety of shitty behaviors: not respecting scope creep boundaries, being overly flirtatious, speaking over people at meetings, taking credit for the member's work and more. Knowing exactly what the problems are can help you make sure the group addresses them properly.

Once you have stated and outlined the problem, it's time to start thinking about the hard part: what to do about it! Is the person lodging the complaint also requesting actions that would make them feel like you're hearing and working on the problem? Do those requests feel proportional and specific? This is a tough one, and I've seen many groups falter here because here in the United States, we have a very carceral understanding of accountability. In our legal system, if you do wrong, you get punished by going to jail. Rather than addressing why the harm happened, we put the person who's been harmed through the hell of a trial, where they are put on the defensive, and we put those who have been declared guilty in prison to "make them pay." In theory, this should mean that after they do their time, they are allowed to put their transgression behind them. In practice, we punish those who are put in the prison industrial complex repeatedly: We don't let them vote, we make it difficult for them to find gainful employment or rent a home. And that's without considering the many ways that racism, sexism, homophobia, transphobia and other kinds of discrimination impact the likelihood that courts will decide a given person is guilty. All these are major flaws in this type of "accountability."

I don't see this method as being an effective form of community accountability in most cases. I think it's attractive in some ways because it gives some people a sense that justice is being served—you harmed me, now I get to harm you back. It also serves to isolate the person who has done harm. They are marked and ostracized, and the community continues forward without them, perhaps for a specific amount of time, perhaps forever. In a group whose members are not invested in each other, this may well feel easier for most of the group. And in certain situations, this may be the only correct approach, like when someone has a clear and directly dangerous pattern of behavior and will not engage in good faith. If they have crossed a clearly stated line, you may not have another safe choice.

Something I've certainly noticed in my years of organizing is that this banishment approach often ignores that an awful lot of labor goes into maintaining a banishment, and the people who often end up forced to do that labor are the harmed parties. If I've kicked someone out of my group for sexual assault, for example, and they go to another group, whose responsibility is it to warn that group's leaders? Do I need to keep tabs on this bad actor? For how long? What about if they've stolen from the group's mutual aid fund? What if that happened five years ago, when they were dealing with addiction, but now they're sober? How invested do I have to be in a person who I have kicked out of my group? Where does my accountability as a leader end? And, of course, what if they really have learned and done the work? Should they be marked forever? Maybe it depends on the problem. But who decides? Unfortunately, a lot of the time, it ends up falling to the person who was impacted by the conflict to keep tabs as the rest of the community loses interest and moves to other issues. This often keeps the harmed person in a state of anxiety and dysregulation rather than allowing them the space to heal.

This is a personal bugbear for me. In my years being a consent educator, I have advised people on how to handle a wide variety of boundary violations. This led to me having the names and reported behaviors of hundreds of people, many from my local community. When community leaders in other communities failed to hold their members accountable, I found myself being a living record of harm, like a sin-eater swallowing the sins of a person so they could die unburdened. When I went to events, people would pull me aside to pour out their troubles, forcing me into the position of being "on the clock" when I was just trying to enjoy a night out. Even when I was not directly involved, it was an incredibly heavy weight that did long-term damage to my mental health. I have to believe there are other, more community-supported options.

Earlier, I talked about a group I organized with whose motto I appreciated: "We have each other's backs, even when we fuck up, especially when we disagree with each other." This is a really tough policy to strive towards! What I appreciated about it though is that it declared non-disposability as a core value, particularly as it was a group of mostly trans people who had felt disposed of by other communities in the past. We agreed to invest in each other, especially when we were upset with each other. Living it meant that we all could build up trust with each other. We didn't always have to agree or get along or even *like* each other, but at the end of the day we were a committed team. Instead of pushing people out when they fucked up, we held them even closer. This not only meant that people were less scared to be told their behavior hurt someone—there was less need to defensively lash out if you weren't afraid of immediately losing your community without any discussion, or afraid of police being weaponized against you—but also, people who had overstepped were held accountable by a group of people who knew what the issue was and were therefore more informed about possible red flags.

This approach works best when the community group using it is relatively small, allowing for that kind of investment and level of familiarity. It may not be the right approach for you, or it may not be practical. I include this example to offer a lesson in why a more transformative justice approach may be a useful tool for resolving conflict. Having an ethical principle that encourages mutual care and mutual accountability allows you to build from a strong core. It gives people a carrot, not a stick. In other words, it's good to find ways you can foster investment in the community and in self-improvement to be a more conscientious member of the community. Additionally, you may find local groups that offer mediation processes, which can loop in a third party to help address and resolve conflict. See the resources section for some suggestions on how to help you educate yourself on accountability processes, so you can adapt them to find something effective for your community.

QUESTIONS

* Can you think of a situation where an activist group you were a part of dealt with tension due to conflict that went unaddressed or was poorly resolved?
    ⊙ What happened, and what do you think would have been a better way to handle it?
    ⊙ How might you handle it differently today?
* Brainstorm some ways a community could talk about conflict productively.
    ⊙ In which situations would this be tough?
    ⊙ How could you address those edge cases?

CHAPTER 13:
LOVE REBELS

Whew. You made it! I made it! It's the end of the book!

I love being an activist, I'm not going to lie. It's in the beating of my heart, in my blood, in my soul. I have been fortunate to see projects I've worked on thrive long beyond me. I've been able to apply things I've learned to organizations that were better off for my experience, which felt rewarding. Seeing injustice and knowing that I did *something* is a core part of who I am, and I wouldn't give that bleeding heart up for any amount of personal peace. I care. I care a lot.

However, my devotion to activism over all else has almost killed me, more than once, because I had no sense of grounding or balance in my life. I have lost sleep, filled with anxiety about what to do about this social issue or that one. I've felt so small and helpless in the face of the great injustices enacted in the world that I didn't think anything I did mattered, but also felt intense pressure, like if I didn't do anything, my community would despise me. I've certainly screamed, "I'm just one fucking person!" into the unfeeling void of the night sky more than once.

When my activism has contributed to me feeling dysregulated, I have learned to stop and just breathe for a minute.

Sitting and checking on my body (Am I hungry? When was the last time I showered?), my mind (How am I feeling? Are my thoughts clear or racing?), and my heart (When did I last hang out with my friends just for fun? Am I doing hobbies that fill my cup?) has become an integral part of my daily life. When I do this, it offers the people around me permission to take care of themselves and each other as well. No one can be "on" all of the time.

It is good to want to change the world! But you will be less effective at doing it if you are reeling internally from crisis to crisis. The tree that cannot bend snaps. Taking care of your tree ensures it's around for years to come. Taking care of other people's trees maintains a healthy and vibrant forest. Earlier in the book I talked a bit about how important shared and individual joy is to balancing activism and healthy relationships. It's not only important in the short term, as a form of stress relief, but also as a vital part of bonding with each other. Fun is a way to remind your loved ones and your community what you're working towards: a better world, with less suffering. Spend some time not only enveloped in what you're fighting against but savoring a glimpse of what you're fighting *for*.

Carving time out for play is good for just taking a break from the harder work, but it's also an important aspect of cognitive well-being! It's great for relieving stress, but it's also useful for stimulating creativity and encouraging you to make new and interesting connections. What play looks like varies from person to person. For me, play involves cooking, baking and gardening—things that may also be daily chores, but ones that I have developed a sense of peaceful mindfulness in doing. Play can also mean reading a book that's just for fun (I love cozy murder mysteries) or watching a comfort TV show. It can be a hobby that you enjoy, like a craft or going for a hike.

It may be something you do with other people, or it might be something special that's just for you.

Even if you're an introvert like I am, it can be important to have some fun time with the people you do activism with as well. One of the things that burns out many collectives is when getting together with your fellow activists fills you with a sense of dread! Playing together allows you all to relax together, which builds up interpersonal relationships and fosters trust. Having fun with each other in between planning and actions is, I believe, the glue that will keep you together when things are rough. Having good times to lean back on can make it easier to have compassion towards each other when you're frustrated.

There are also ways to engage in activism that can help you reconnect with the inherent joy of helping. I had a wonderful time crocheting squares for a quilt alongside many other people, to be stitched together and gifted to someone we cared about who was hospitalized. You could throw a rent party for someone who is struggling to make ends meet or do a performance event with a raffle to raise money for refugees. One of my favorite examples of this concept is an antifascist fashion show. My fellow activists put together cyberpunk-inspired "Antifa fashion" for a makeshift runway, with live music and a bake sale. We raised funds for our own street medic supplies and gave some away to other causes that needed financial support, and it was a lot of fun to do! Laughing and goofing off together didn't take away from the serious work, but it helped us fan the flames of our passion to do it.

I also want to again underline that pacing yourself is important. I would always rather people do small things consistently than one big thing that burns them out so badly they never organize again! If you need a break, you can and should take one. If you rest up, you'll be able to re-enter the fight when you are strengthened again. Ask people for help.

Signal boost ways for them to step up. Collaborate with other projects so you can step back from planning. Mutual aid is so varied, and there are many ways to contribute that will allow you to spend time with your friends and family. Only you know the right balance to fill your cup.

I named this book *Love Rebels* because I wanted to encourage people to be a love rebel, to reimagine what loving each other and loving ourselves means. To be a love rebel is to recognize the radical potential of fostering *agape*—a Greek word meaning the conscious decision to love others without demanding something in return. In a world that seems constantly determined to encourage us to divide, to push away, to be suspicious of each other, choosing love—hard, messy, transformative, fierce, compassionate, patient and mindful love—is maybe one of the most radical things you can do.

I also chose *Love Rebels* because I think love is inherently rebellious. Perhaps it's my current philosophical obsession with Albert Camus (who I named my cat after), who believed humans were meant to absurdly seek meaning in their lives, conscious that they were in a world that offered no such meaning. I think that love reminds us to care—about each other, about the impact of social dynamics, about "a better life" of some kind. To choose love is to embrace our humanity, complex as it is. Without love, why rebel? Love is, I believe, inherently about hope and faith, giving us something to fight for.

I hope that my words in this book have offered you some solace, have helped you feel seen and less alone. I think sometimes that as activists, we expect ourselves to be strong and independent all the time, knowing exactly what to say and when to act. But we are soft, vulnerable, confused creatures even as we're simultaneously defenders of the downtrodden and seekers of justice. I wrote this book to remind you that self-care is community care, community care is self-care, and everyone needs a break sometimes. There are plenty of things to do, and they'll still be there tomorrow.

We must have bread, and we must have roses, too. I hope you have found both here. Thank you for reading.

GLOSSARY

There are many ways to define the concepts in this book and you may have a different interpretation of some. Here is a brief summary of each in my own words, from my perspective.

Accountability: Taking ownership of your choices and actions without defensiveness. Often, accountability is a combination of acknowledgment in words, changing behaviors and making amends in clearly defined ways when appropriate.

Boundaries: A clear space or limit between you and another person, where you begin and others end. Boundaries can be physical, emotional, time-based, sexual or material. They can be how close you're willing to get to someone else, and also where you draw the line. A "soft" boundary is one that's a little flexible or fuzzy, while a "hard" boundary is clear cut.

Calling In: Telling someone that something they said or did was harmful in private. Calling in can be effective when there is trust that your individual disapproval is enough to encourage change, as it feels a little gentler than calling out. However, it requires more of your time and labor as you are on your own, and power dynamics can make it uncomfortable if the person doing the calling in has less clout.

Calling Out: Telling someone that something they said or did was harmful in public. Calling out can be effective when calling in did not work, when you feel you need witnesses to your call for accountability or to demonstrate the community's disapproval. Calling someone out can lead to defensiveness and aggression on the part of the person being called out, and it can lead to uneven consequences that end up impacting marginalized people more.

Consent Culture: A social structure focusing on increasing the opportunities for people to opt in (or opt out) of situations. Consent culture is about moving towards centering consent in interactions, rather than avoiding violation. It's about treating autonomy as sacrosanct and boundaries as valuable information to be respected.

Entitlement Culture: A social structure where we arrogantly operate under the impression that other people "owe us" unreasonable privileges. I prefer to use this term instead of "rape culture" because I feel it more accurately gets to the root of the problem: people with social advantages feeling they deserve something from others because of that power.

Marginalization: When certain groups of people are denied access to basic services or opportunities because they are deemed powerless or unimportant. This often goes hand in hand with discrimination, particularly for minorities, and can be related to ethnicity, economic circumstance, gender, sexual orientation, immigration status, physical or mental ability, weight, age and many more factors. Often, people who are marginalized experience multiple points of marginalization.

Rape Culture: A social structure wherein sexual violence (particularly against people who experience misogyny) is normalized, excused away and dismissed—in the media, in the legal system and/or in the culture at large. Often in a rape culture, victims are blamed for their assaults and the onus is on avoiding rape instead of on potential rapists not abusing people.

Red Flag: A warning sign that something needs to be dealt with or that there is a problem to be addressed. While this term is often used for assessing others (especially in relationships), in this book I use it to encourage recognizing your own, internal red flags that tell you that something isn't right. This could be a queasy feeling in your gut or finding yourself avoiding an interaction. It isn't necessarily a dealbreaker in this context, but rather a sign to stop and reflect on how you feel, what's going on and what you need.

Scrupulosity: Overwhelming guilt and anxiety over moral issues, to the point of emotional distress, compulsive behaviors and social impairment.

Social Advantages: Special, unasked for and unearned positive treatment/value offered only to specific groups by nature of their identity (or perceived identity). It is the counterpart to marginalization. Also called "privilege."

Transformative Justice: An ideal about justice that offers the possibility that someone who does harm can learn, feel empathy and seek to be accountable for that harm. It seeks to center the victim and give them an active role offering input into the process, rather than relying on an outside corrupt criminal justice system that prefers punishment, retribution and stigma. Transformative justice is an ideal to work towards, in my opinion, rather than a concrete formula.

Triggers: Reminders of past trauma, often leading to re-experiencing that trauma in some capacity. Triggers vary wildly and can be internally or externally expressed through disassociation, flashbacks and distress. Triggers are often referred to in relation to substance abuse or PTSD, but they can also be related to other mental health issues.

RESOURCES

HOW TO ASK FOR HELP

So, something big, and scary, or sad, or angering has happened. We feel helpless, hopeless in the face of this thing. We know we are not alone, yet we feel completely isolated in the experience of this thing. Frantically, we reach out for help from our loved ones and/or our community. We are vulnerable, we are raw in our ask. And people respond, "Of course, just let us know what you need!"

It's absolutely a fair response. The problem is that for many of us, it's difficult if not impossible to figure out what we feel, never mind what we need. It was hard enough to ask for help in the first place! And so, we quietly accept whatever help people thrust upon us, knowing that it's well-intentioned, even if it doesn't feel helpful to us. Or maybe we just withdraw, and say, yeah, sure, I'll get back to you, and by the time we've dealt with the immediate trauma it's been a couple of weeks, and we no longer feel comfortable following up. Our loved ones feel frustrated that they couldn't be of service, and we feel alone, even as we know how unfair that is.

I've definitely scolded myself in those moments, like how dare I ask my friends to read my mind and give me what I need when I don't even know what I need myself! But that response doesn't actually help anything. I've thought about how sometimes when I go to a restaurant, I don't know what I want until I see a photo of it. Seeing the options clearly made decision-making far easier and more efficient. What if I could do that, but for acts of service and showing up? I started making up a list of things I could look at when in that numb state of crisis and instability to help me decide what I needed. I'd look through my list and consider what felt stressful, what felt like a relief and what didn't make me feel anything at all. Then, I could provide people with a short list of the kinds of help I was looking for.

It was incredible. People were far more likely to show up for me when they knew exactly what I was asking for. I needed a meal? Done. I needed someone to call when I was grieving? Easy. I needed someone to make me a playlist of music for my mood? No problem. By having a variety of ways that people could show up for me that I genuinely wanted, some that cost money, some that cost time, I was able to meet my needs and feel the love of those around me. And they felt like they were making a positive impact. Win-win.

Here's my list, which I encourage you to use as a starting place for your own. This is, of course, not appropriate for all people in all moments with all of the people they may ask for help, but hopefully it will stir up some thoughts so you can make your own menu of emotionally supportive acts. You may be surprised at who shows up when you do this. I've had people I rarely hang out with show up out of the blue to be my biggest cheerleaders during times of crisis.

THE HELP LIST

What do you need right now?
Over the next week?

* Advice
* Sympathy
* Someone to
  listen to you
* Food
* A chore handled
* A plan created
* Time alone
* Time with
  another person
* Time with a group
* Being at home
* Being away
  from home
* A distraction
* Doing something
  familiar/comforting
* Trying something
  new
* A physical activity
* A fun activity
* Money
* A referral

* A list of resources
* A book that
  might help
* Time with animals
* Time with children
* In-person time
* A phone call
* A video chat
* Physical contact
* Emotional presence
* Regular text check-
  ins (Also, define
  regular! Every
  day? Once a week?)
* Listening to music
* Time in nature
* Sensual touch
* Cuddling
* Massage
* Meditation
* Dance

* Add your own!

FURTHER READING

I personally do not agree with everything presented in these resources, but I think they are useful in helping people think critically about the topic at hand. Some are about community activism, some are about marginalized communities, some are about consent culture. I think there's something to gain in them all, and they've all informed my beliefs. And there's much more out there!

Consent Culture

* Captain Awkward: Excellent advice on communication and boundary setting. captainawkward.com
* Consent Culture US: The website created by Kitty Stryker to set the tone of what consent culture means and how to work towards it. consentculture.com
* Consent Culture UK: The website created by Jenn Wilson, founder of the International Day of Consent (#IDoConsent, November 30). consentculture.co.uk and idoconsent.org
* *Energetic Boundaries: How to Stay Protected and Connected in Work, Love, and Life* by Cyndi Dale
* Glow West: A podcast that explores sex, sexuality and the body from a sexual wellness perspective, hosted by Dr. Caroline West. glowwest.org
* *Learning Good Consent: Building Ethical Relationships in a Complicated World* by Cindy Crabb
* Nurturing Human Touch: A starting place for exploring consent and touch. nurturinghumantouch.com
* *Pleasure Activism: The Politics of Feeling Good* by adrienne maree brown

* *Polysecure: Attachment, Trauma and Consensual Nonmonogamy* by Jessica Fern
* *Sexual Revolution: Modern Fascism and the Feminist Fightback* by Laurie Penny
* *Speaking from the Heart: 18 Languages for Modern Love* by Anne Hodder-Shipp
* *The Art of Receiving and Giving* by Betty Martin with Robyn Dalzen
* *The Body Is Not An Apology: The Power of Radical Self-Love* by Sonya Renee Taylor
* *Tomorrow Sex Will Be Good Again: Women and Desire in the Age of Consent* by Katherine Angel
* *Unfuck Your Boundaries: Build Better Relationships Through Consent, Communication, and Expressing Your Needs* by Faith G. Harper
* *We Can't All be Abolitionist and Conflict Avoidants* by Erotics of Liberation
* *Yes Means Yes!: Visions of Female Sexual Power and A World Without Rape* by Jaclyn Friedman and Jessica Valenti

Community Organizing

* Activist Handbook: Online resources and a living library of strategies, tactics and tools. activisthandbook.org
* *And the Band Played On: Politics, People, and the AIDS Epidemic* by Randy Shilts
* *A Paradise Built in Hell: The Extraordinary Communities That Arise in Disaster* by Rebecca Solnit
* *Beautiful Trouble: A Toolbox for Revolution,* assembled by Andrew Boyd

* *Beyond Survival: Strategies and Stories from the Transformative Justice Movement*, edited by Leah Lakshmi Piepzna-Samarasinha and Ejeris Dixon
* Crimethinc: A library of resources with tools, personal experiences and activist histories. crimethinc.com/library
* *Difficult Conversations: How to Discuss What Matters Most* by Douglas Stone, Bruce Patton and Sheila Heen
* *Excluded: Making Feminist and Queer Movements More Inclusive* by Julia Serano
* *Fumbling Towards Repair: A Workbook for Community Accountability Facilitators* by Mariame Kaba and Shira Hassan
* *Hegemony How-To: A Road Map for Radicals* by Jonathan Smucker
* *In It Together: Navigating Depression with Partners, Friends, and Family* by JoEllen Notte
* INCITE!: Radical feminists of color organizing around ending state violence in their communities, thorough resources on community accountability. incite-national.org
* *Joyful Militancy: Building Thriving Resistance in Toxic Times* by carla bergman and Nick Montgomery.
* Non-Monogamy Help: A relationship advice podcast for people in nonmonogamous or polyamorous relationships hosted by Lola Phoenix. nonmonogamyhelp.libsyn.com
* *Overcoming Burnout* by Nicole Rose
* *Rest is Resistance: A Manifesto* by Tricia Hersey
* *Robert's Rules Simplified* by Arthur T. Lewis and Henry M. Robert.
* *Starting Somewhere: Community Organizing for Socially Awkward People Who've Had Enough* by Roderick Douglass
* *Surviving the Future: Abolitionist Queer Strategies*, edited by Shuli Branson, Raven Hudson and Bry Reed

* *Teaching to Transgress: Education as the Practice of Freedom* by bell hooks
* The Citizen's Handbook: A collection of articles to help you engage your community in a variety of ways. citizenshandbook.org/toc.html
* The Commons Library: 1000+ online articles on creative activism, campaign strategy, accountability and more. commonslibrary.org
* The Ex-Worker: An anarchist podcast dealing with various ideas and actions. This episode is specifically about community accountability: crimethinc. com/podcasts/the-ex-worker/episodes/8
* *The Revolution Starts at Home*, edited by Ching-In Chen, Jai Dulani and Leah Lakshmi Piepzna-Samarasinha
* Totally Not Malware (Resources for Activists): A practical collection of information on operational security, protest first aid and other sensible advice. blog.totallynotmalware.net/?cat=26
* Unlocking Us: A podcast about deeply personal topics including shame, accountability, vulnerability and more hosted by Brené Brown. brenebrown.com/ podcast/brene-on-shame-and-accountability
* *We Do This 'Til We Free Us: Abolitionist Organizing and Transforming Justice* by Mariame Kaba

Anti-Oppression Work and Education
* American Sex Podcast: An AASECT award-winning podcast dedicated to changing America's dysfunctional relationship with sex hosted by Sunny Megatron. americansexpodcast.com
* *An Indigenous Peoples' History of the United States* by Roxanne Dunbar-Ortiz

* Beau of the Fifth Column: A YouTube channel run by a Southern journalist with unique insight into politics, mutual aid and current events. youtube.com/c/BeauoftheFifthColumn
* *Black Skin, White Masks* by Frantz Fanon
* *Care Work: Dreaming Disability Justice* by Leah Lakshmi Piepzna-Samarasinha
* *Coming Out Like A Porn Star: Essays On Pornography, Protection, and Privacy*, edited by Jiz Lee
* *Fight Like Hell: The Untold History of American Labor* by Kim Kelly
* "From White Racist to White Anti-Racist": An article by Tema Okun to help white people understand their identity as white people within a racist system. fammed.wisc.edu/files /webfm-uploads/documents/diversity/LifeLongJourney.pdf
* *Gender Euphoria*, edited by Laura Kate Dale
* *Hood Feminism: Notes from the Women That a Movement Forgot* by Mikki Kendall
* *I Hope We Choose Love* by Kai Cheng Thom
* *Jesus and John Wayne: How White Evangelicals Corrupted a Faith and Fractured a Nation* by Kristin Kobes Du Mez
* *Love's Not Color Blind: Race and Representation in Polyamorous and Other Alternative Communities* by Kevin A. Patterson
* *Revolting Prostitutes* by Juno Mac and Molly Smith
* *Sister Outsider: Essays and Speeches* by Audre Lorde
* *So You Want to Talk About Race* by Ijeoma Oluo
* *The Exvangelicals: Loving, Living, and Leaving the White Evangelical Church* by Sarah McCammon
* Tits and Sass: Writing by sex workers for sex workers about topics including survival sex work, disability and sex work in a pandemic. titsandsass.com
* *Uncomfortable Labels* by Laura Kate Dale

Crisis Resources

* First Response to Sexual Assault: A flyer with good advice if you find yourself triaging a sexual assault survivor. fris. org/Resources/PDFs/Brochures/Bro-FirstRespond.pdf
* Kink Aware Professionals: Therapists, doctors and other professionals who have experience with alternative relationships, organized by the National Coalition for Sexual Freedom. kapprofessionals.org
* National Domestic Violence Hotline: A 24/7 hotline with an extensive resource list organized by state. 1–800–799–SAFE (7233) or TTY 1–800–787–3224 thehotline.org
* Gay Men's Domestic Violence Project: A 24/7 hotline that supports victims and survivors through education, advocacy and direct services. 1–800–832–1901
* The Trevor Project: Free, trained crisis counselors focused on LGBTQ+ youth, available 24/7 via hotline or chat. 1–866–488–7386 thetrevorproject.org/get-help
* Trans Lifeline: Trans peer support hotline by and for trans folks. US: 1–877–565–8860, Canada: 1–877–330–6366 https://translifeline.org

INDEX

Also from Thornapple Press

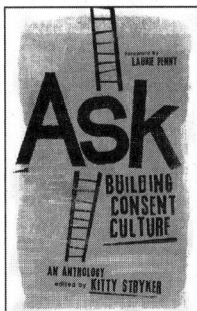

Ask: Building Consent Culture

Edited by Kitty Stryker
with a foreword by Laurie Penny

"There are certain conversations that deepen how you think; positively impact how you act; expand your view and understanding of the world, and forever alter how you approach it. This book is full of them. Make room for it—then spread the word."
—Alix Fox, journalist, sex educator and ambassador for the Brook sexual wellbeing charity

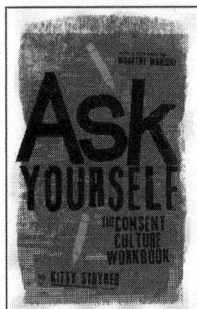

Ask Yourself: The Consent Culture Workbook

Kitty Stryker, with a foreword by Wagatwe Wanjuki

"Ask: Building Consent Culture editor Kitty Stryker invites readers to delve deeper, with guest experts and personal anecdotes, to manifest a culture of consent in one's own community that starts at the heart."
—Jiz Lee, editor of *Coming Out Like a Porn Star*

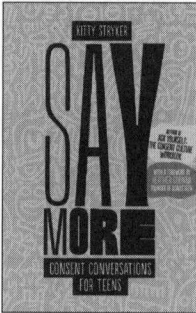

Say More:
Consent Conversations for Teens

Kitty Stryker, with a foreword by
Heather Corinna

"Don't be fooled into thinking this book is just for teens. It's terrific for adults too. In a rare combination of clarity and nuance, it's useful for everyone. And it's a joy to read."

—Dr. Betty Martin, author of
The Art of Receiving and Giving:
the Wheel of Consent

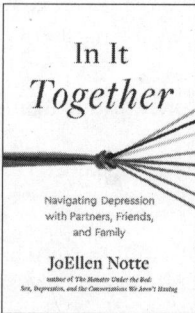

In It Together: Navigating Depression with Partners, Friends, and Family

JoEllen Notte

"Am I allowed to say I laughed and had so much fun reading about depression? Read this book and you'll feel seen—and you'll walk away with a real-life guide to helping loved ones without sacrificing your own mental health."

—Meredith Goldstein, Boston Globe
Love Letters advice columnist,
podcast host and author of
Can't Help Myself

ABOUT THE AUTHOR

Kitty Stryker is a writer, activist and authority on developing a consent culture in alternative communities. She is the founder of consentculture.com, a hub for LGBTQ+, kinky and polyamorous folks looking for a sex-critical approach to relationships and was one of the first people to talk about what a consent culture was and could be. She's the editor of *Ask: Building Consent Culture* and the author of *Ask Yourself: The Consent Culture Workbook* and *Say More: Consent Conversations for Teens.* Kitty is especially interested in bringing conversations about consent out of the bedroom and into everyday life.

This page intentionally left blank for burning.

This page intentionally left blank for burning.